The Mafia in Sicilian Literature

Published and Forthcoming by New Academia Publishing

HERETICAL EM[PIRICISM
by Pierpaolo Pasolini; Ben Lawton and Louise K. Barnett, eds., trs.

PIER PAOLO PASOLINI: 30 Years Later
Ben Lawton, ed.

RIVERS OF FIRE: Mythic Themes in Homer's Iliad
by Chris J. Mackie

SUPER/HEROES: From Hercules to Superman
Wendy Haslem, Angela Ndalianis and Chris Mackie, eds.

ON THE ROAD TO BAGHDAD, or TRAVELING BICULTURALISM: Theorizing a Bicultural Approach to Contemporary World Fiction
Gönul Pultar, ed.

IMAGING RUSSIA 2000: Film and Facts
by Anna Lawton (CHOICE Outstanding Academic Title 2005)

BEFORE THE FALL: Soviet Cinema in The Gorbachev Years
by Anna Lawton

RUSSIAN FUTURISM: A History
by Vladimir Markov

WORDS IN REVOLUTION: Russian Futurist Manifestoes 1912-1928
Anna Lawton and Herbert Eagle, eds., trs.

VISUAL CULTURE IN SHANGHAI, 1850s-1930s
Jason C. Kuo, ed.

LIVING NOVELS: A Journey through Twentieth-Century Fiction
by Sascha Talmor

FROM THE HOLY LAND TO THE NEW JERUSALEM: Specialness, Utopia, and Holocaust
by Arthur Grenke

GOD, GREED, AND GENOCIDE: The Holocaust through the Centuries
by Arthur Grenke

To read an excerpt, visit: www.newacademia.com

The Mafia
in Sicilian Literature

Corinna del Greco Lobner

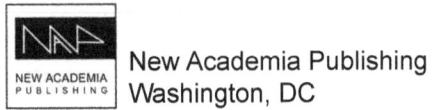
New Academia Publishing
Washington, DC

Copyright © 2007 by Corinna del Greco Lobner

New Academia Publishing, 2008

All rights reserved. No part of this book may be reproduced or transmitted in any form or by any means, electronic or mechanical, including photocopying, recording, or by any information storage and retrieval system.

Printed in the United States of America

Library of Congress Control Number: 2008921866
ISBN 978-0-9800814-5-9 paperback (alk. paper)

New Academia Publishing, LLC
P.O. Box 27420
Washington, DC 20038-7420
www.newacademia.com - info@newacademia.com

For Wesley F. Lobner, who loved Sicily

*If we want things to stay as they are,
things will have to change.*

Giuseppe Tomasi di Lampedusa, *The Leopard*

Contents

Foreword   x

Acknowledgements   xi

I. What is the Mafia?   1

II. Sicilian History: A Merger of Fire and Ice   23

III. The Mafia in Sicilian Literature: Beginnings   37

IV. Lust, Vengeance and Honor   49

V. The Rise of the Mafia in Sicily's Historical Novel: Pirandello, De Roberto, Lampedusa   67

VI. The Defeat of Reason: Sciascia and Power   91

VII. Los Angeles, 1941-1942   125

Notes   130

Works cited   135

Foreword

Sicilian writer Leonard Sciascia in *Le parrocchie di Regalpetra* explains: "All my books are only one. A book about Sicily that touched the sorrowful trail of the past and the present and that articulates itself like the history of a continuous defeat of reason and of those that in this defeat were... overcome and annihilated." * Sciascia knew his world, its most intimate secrets and the mind of the Sicilians taught by centuries of invasions and hardships to rely only on themselves and extended family ties. Although not all the literary works presented here have been translated into English, it is hoped that readers will be able to follow the labyrinthian nature of the Mafia and its lasting power as recorded by some of Sicily's greatest writers.

Acknowledgements

I am indebted to the University of Tulsa for giving me the opportunity to pursue my research on the Mafia in Sicily, and for the chance to teach several classes on the topic. My students helped me to gather further information and to consider situations I had not addressed. My deepest appreciation goes to Dr. Brian Murray, Professor of English and Journalism at Jesuit College in Baltimore, for the time he spent in reviewing the original manuscript and making needed suggestions. I am also indebted to my colleagues at the University of Tulsa, Dr. Carol Kealiher, Associate Editor of Academic Publications, Professor Thomas Benediktson, Dean of Arts and Letters and Dr. Victor Udwin, Professor of German and Comparative Literature for their support and for their insightful suggestions. My daughter, Gloria Lobner Standeford, and her husband, Rob Standeford, were extremely helpful in defining and solving computer problems while the work was in progress. Professor Thomas F. Staley, Director of the Harry Ransom Humanities Research Center at the University of Texas in Austin, encouraged the progress of this work all along. Kay Huculak's expert help in finalizing and making the book ready for publication, her enthusiasm and expertise, can't be acknowledged enough. Last, but far from least, my sincere appreciation goes to the amici degli amici, friends of friends, who met with me every day in Palermo at a small bar near the port. Omertà forbids me to mention their names. Even so, their help was invaluable.

I

What is the Mafia?

The Mafia has long been a source of public fascination. Hollywood made its debut in organized crime in 1912 with D. W. Griffith's *The Musketeers of Pig Alley* and championed the genre again in 1922-23 with *Dr. Mabuse and The Gambler* (Parts I and II), directed by Fritz Lang. Both dramas centered on a criminal boss, evil but charismatic. *Underworld* (1927) directed by Josef Von Sternberg signaled a remarkable first by presenting the mobster's point of view. The film earned many accolades, among these the "Best Story Award" for Ben Hecht. During the 1930s and 1940s Italian-American gangster films turned into a thrilling cult of killers engaged in a ruthless quest for power and money. *Little Caesar* (1930), starring Edward G. Robinson as Rico Bandello, an alias for Al Capone, was followed by Howard Hawks's *Scarface: The Shame of a Nation* (1932). Paul Muni was Tony Camonte, another alias for Capone. The film introduced machine guns allowing the carnage on screen to reach epic proportions with a total of twenty-eight victims. Richard Thorpe's *The Black Hand* (1950), New York's local version of the Sicilian Mafia, resumed the trend while Terence Young's *Joe Valachi* (1972) dramatized the mobster's revelations of *Cosa Nostra's* secrets to a congressional committee. American appetite for mob stories reached its zenith that year with Francis Coppola's *The Godfather* based on Mario Puzo's best selling novel. The film's phenomenal success was partly due to its emotional appeal. Marlon Brando as Don Corleone and Al Pacino as his son succeeded in conveying the strong family bond that made the saga of Sicilian-American immigrants especially appealing. *The Godfather* gave a perceptive rendition of what Sicilians call *sentire* Mafioso ("Mafioso feeling") an expression that conveys the blend of native pride and the resentment for governmental intrusion in family business that throughout history made the Mafia the only organization Sicilians could trust to protect their individual rights. Today *The Sopranos* revives an interest in Mafioso exploits and makes HBO's weekly series a must watch. As Steve Busceni, occasional director of *The Sopranos* makes clear, the reason Tony Soprano (James Gandolfini) scores high notes with TV viewers lies in the intense emotional impact of the character often compelled to perform murderous deeds to keep intact the family's reputation and its hold on the business.

While *The Sopranos* offers an exceptional study of Mafia assimilation to the American way of life, the cultural and historical circumstances that shaped the Mafia in Sicily are quite different. Italian experts on the Sicilian Mafia generally agree that the *onorata società* ("honorable society") commonly known as Mafia, started in Sicily's *latifondi*, ("rural communities") as a safeguard against abusive local absentee landlords–mostly aristocrats–who eventually were expropriated and replaced by their clever Mafiosi administrators or *campieri*. The administrators made it their business to take advantage of the powerless farm hands that depended on them to make their living. Sicilian Mafia scholar Giovanni Cucinotta writes:

> "The Baron who considered the administration of the feud and dealing with farm workers below his dignity, sent an administrator known as campiere [field supervisor] to defend and oversee his property. The stipend of the campiere was provided half by the owner and half by the farm hands. He also received a share of the land that he either tilled for himself or sublet to another party. His privileged position allowed the campiere to accumulate a capital and, as a

What is the Mafia? 3

consequence, to become part of a small group of landowners. Yet, how could the campiere who was, after all, little more than a farm hand achieve, stabilize and increase his newly acquired social status? By the use of violence. What was needed to advance from plain farm hand to campiere was not intelligence or education, but physical courage, open criminal tendencies and, most of all, the ability to suppress the rebellion of others like him. In conclusion, to be a guard for a landowner was to be a Mafioso. In the feudal system, violence was the supreme ruler. It is here [in feudal land] that we find bandits, thieves, along with farm workers. The campiere strikes a deal with the bandits, stipulates an agreement with the thieves and kills the rest." [1]

This is only the beginning of a social system that from the end of the 18th century to the beginning of the 19th century led to a tax known as *gabella*, a form of taxation paid to the state for merchandise brought in from another territory. It was enforced by the *gabelloti* ("tax collectors") who worked for the Barons exploiting the farm hands and appropriating the largest share of the income for their own use. The *gabelloto* (singular form of *gabelloti*) was not officially a criminal. By recycling stolen cattle and other merchandise, however, he made huge profits gaining prestige and consolidating his powerful hold on the economy. It is a chain-link of exploitation prompted by the accumulation of goods or *la roba* that becomes an end in it.

Amassing riches and passing them on to the family is the object of every Mafioso who reaches his goal by embracing *omertà* ("code of silence"), and following the rules prescribed by the *padrino* ("godfather") in charge of the *cosca* ("family"). By the way, *cosca* in Sicilian dialect means 'artichoke'—in Italian the vegetable is called *carciofo*. When Italian newspapers refer to *politica del carciofo* ("politics of the artichoke"), they are referring to politics of the Mafia. Henner Hess[2] relates that Antonino Cutrera, in his early work *La Mafia e I Mafiosi, Origine e Manifestazioni*,[3] explains:

"Each group of Mafiosi is allegorically represented by an artichoke whose trunk stands for the leader while its leaves stand for his followers. In fact, is quite common to describe a man regarded as a valuable person as *lu trunzu ri l'omini* ("the trunk of the man"). The name *cosca* likens the Mafioso leader and the men grouped around him to the leaves of the artichoke."

Because of its unique system of reciprocal dependency, the Sicilian Mafia calls for a special set of references marked by secrecy and minimal vocal communication or what Sicilians call *mezza parola* ("half a word"). Glances and intuition are the most effective means to reach mutual understanding. A progressive evolution of the means to secure *la roba* shows the Mafia's exceptional adaptability to the passage of time. The role of the Mafioso in Sicily's history links the Mafioso way of life to the traditions of the Sicilians so as to make the Mafia an in disguisable cultural manifestation; however, the Sicilians insist there is a distinction Mafia and mafia. The Mafia refers to Mafioso as "the people who belong to organized crime," and the second distinction is of a mafioso a "person who is proud to be Sicilian."

Giovanni Cucinotta points out: "once more today we hear a distinction between 'old' and 'new' Mafia. It's difficult to know, however, or to explain where the 'old' starts and where the 'new'; begins."[4] In spite of necessary adjustments to differing economic, political circumstances "the soul" of the Mafia has not changed. Cucinotta explains that there has been "an evolution" not a "revolution" which has increased its power. Machiavellian to extremes and thus profitably opportunistic, the Mafia's motto all along has been "change with continuity,"[5] which points to the necessity of flexibility according to the situation. Such attitude demands a closer collaboration with the government in Rome and extensive agreements with other European countries including the American Mafia. Although it is simplistic to reduce the Mafia to a formula, the latest definition given by the Italian government is "multinational of crime." The fulcrum of operations today is in Naples, where the *Camorra* (Neapolitan counterpart of the Sicilian Mafia) creates constant problems with drug trafficking and gang murders.[6] Rome is actively contributing to Mafia power through a solidly installed bureaucratic system where the Mafia operates within a legal framework that occasionally includes the Vatican. Regions in central Italy do their part by transferring Mafia money through bank transactions. Thus *denaro nero* ("black or dirty money") is deposited and becomes quietly absorbed by banks uninterested in the provenience. Ironically, there are times when large amounts of this money are assigned to public buildings such as schools, hospitals, and sport arenas, even churches. Milan, one of Italy's foremost centers of business transactions, is pivotal to Mafia interests and has become a prosperous target for mob operations since the end of World War II.

Understanding this common Mafia jargon helps to achieve a closer perspective in the activities of the *onorata società* ("honorable society") while gaining more familiarity with the assorted blend of historical and cultural factors that rule Sicilian life. These particular terms give further insight into the structural, and the cultural counterparts that make the Mafia unique. Terms defining the Mafioso's behavior offer important clues about how the Mafia assigns roles to its members. *Pizzu*, for instance, is a tax prison inmates impose on newcomers to secure protection from dangerous surprises. Today, Italy and the United States still use *Pizzu*. *Cadavere eccellente* ("excellent corpse") indicates a prominent victim of the Mafia such as a *cornuto* ("cuckold")–the worst insult for a Sicilian–is occasionally used as a pretext to eliminate rival Mafiosi falsely accused of illicit relations with the murderer's wife. *'Ngiuria* ("a blemish in the features") is an unmistakable mark of identification in the appearance of the individual that makes him recognizable. *Vendetta trasversale* ("vengeance across the line") implies the slaughter of every member of the Mafioso's blood family regardless of its innocence, while its opposite, *vittoria trasversale* ("victory across the line") refers to victory over a rival *cosca* ("family"). *Commissione* is the name of the Mafia's high command. *Baccaglio* is Sicilian criminal jargon used in prison; *annacari* ("swaggering") is a Mafioso-style walk they use in religious processions. *Colletti bianchi* ("white collars") is someone with a desk job who leads a life within the law; bank employees working with the Mafia qualify for this category. A *Combinato* ("combined") is someone who has been initiated into *Cosa Nostra* ("Our Thing") as compared to its opposite *dissociato*. *Galantuomo* ("honest man") is a respected, well to do citizen who uses his power to increase his wealth and oversees business deals. *Malacarni* (Sicilian for "evil flesh") is someone who will commit any kind of evil or a betrayer. *Omu de panza* ("man with a belly") is a man who knows how to keep quiet and a *Pentitó* is a repentant Mafioso who "sings" to the cops to save his skin. *Picciottu is* a boy who aspires to become a *picciottu onoratu*, a 'boy with honor,' also called *soldato* ("soldier"). The boy must prove his courage by committing a murder before he becomes a "made man," a full member of the Mafia. Because of its system of promotions within the organization, the Mafia retains a collegiate structure advancing those candidates who show aptitude to succeed. As a rule the Sicilian family disposes of fifty members ranked in military order. The *soldato* can be promoted to *capo decina*, literally 'commander of ten,' and eventually to *capo-mandamento* a further step toward the summit of the Mafia, the Commission or Cupola. A *consigliore*, a trustworthy man of honor with exceptional mediating skills, functions as an advisor to the *padrino* ("godfather") and is not usually a lawyer as often surmised in American Mafia fiction. *Uomo d'onore posato* is a 'man of honor put down' and is expelled from *Cosa Nostra*. *Sbirro*, 'jailer' in archaic Italian, in Mafia jargon means 'policeman.' *Uomini qualificati* (also known as *specialisti*), are Mafia members assigned to specialized tasks such as money laundering. *Uomo rispettato* translates into 'a Mafioso who holds a high post in the hierarchy of power.'

To understand fully the Mafia's hold on the imagination of the public, it's useful to examine the way Italian cinema has approached the problem after World War II, often making the Mafioso a symbol of resistance against government intrusion. Some of these pictures have been inspired by government indifference to the economic and social plight of Sicily and of southern Italy. Yet, in contemporary cinema, the direction seems to be changing. Courageous movie producers and directors are exposing risky endeavors that were staged by the Mafia. One of them, Michele Pantaleone, has had several unpleasant encounters with the Mafia because of their substantial investments in commercial films. Pantaleone has authored various reports on the subject, his best known,[7] *Mafia e droga*, exposes the danger of producing a film on the Mafia. It is not rare for a producer to run into unusual complications. Sometimes, a producer is offered protection and, on occasion, is forced to hire collaborators or interpreters who are under the protection of *amici* ("friends"). When a movie concerning the real Mafia–as portrayed in Benigni's comic film, *Johnny Stecchino*–the producer has a reason to be nervous. Pantaleone explains that there are two scenarios that follow the proposal: either the producer ends the conversation with a quip aimed at his collaborators, "What if they shoot us?" or he considers the project but refuses to give an answer until the Italian Ministry of Entertainment has assured the distribution of the film through an agency that only on occasion grants a minimal income guarantee for risky ventures called *Italnoleggio*. Pantaleone speaks from experience. In order to finance a film based on his book *Mafia e droga*, he postponed filming until the government agreed to subsidize the project.

Don Masino Buscetta, the most reliable *pentito* (a man who "sings") in recent years, explains that a great deal of the mystique surrounding the organization of Mafia is a literary creation. The real Mafiosi, Buscetta explains, are simply "honorable" men. In big cities like Palermo each man of honor belongs to a *borgata* ("neighborhood") while in smaller centers the *cosca* ("family") takes its name from the locality—Corleone, for example. Although these terms are important in understanding Mafia cultures, readers of Sicilian literature should keep in mind that the above terms are rarely introduced in a narrative context, but present by implication. Sicilian writer Leonardo Sciascia relies on *omertà* ("code of silence") as stylistic device challenging readers to discover the truth hidden in the text. According to Sciascia, prerequisites for the reader eager to gain a full understanding of the plot are knowledge of Sicilian history and the ability to recognize and solve the clues often planted in his novels. For instance, in *The Day of the Owl* a dog's name *Barriccieddu* or *Bargieddu* is a corrupted form of *bargello*. These names refer to an officer in the Republic of Florence who is the commander of the police and, chief of the *sbirri* ("jailers") who is responsible for torturing the prisoners. Thus, the name of the officer becomes a symbol of persecution, while the owl in the title is another symbol of betrayal, this time via Shakespeare.[8]

Sciascia suggests *La Mafia*, a comedy by Giovanni Alfredo Cesareo staged in Sicily during WWI for readers interested in finding the best indicator of *sentire Mafioso* ("Mafioso feeling"). In the play the local *capomafia* ("head of mafia") Don Rasconà, a powerful *cacicco* ("mediator"), gives a point–by–point explanation of this historical–cultural paradigm. The arguments he presents are essential to the understanding of the resentment Sicilians feel for mainlanders (Italians from the peninsula), a sentiment largely responsible for the persistent identification of the Mafia with *Sicilianità*, an insular patriotic response to the oppression of Italy's central government dating from Sicily's annexation from the mainland in 1861. *La Mafia* is the classic story of love and parental disapproval. The boy's influential father, Baron Montedomini, will not consent to his son's marriage with the daughter of an Italian government official. The young people elope, and the solution to the crisis is brought about by Don Rasconà, seemingly eager to reconcile the two parties but looking out for his personal gain. The implied reward for his services will be the cooperation of the father of the bride who, in his position of government representative in Italy, will find himself forced to carry out Mafia policies. Don Rasconà's position as mediator is revealed in the play by his explanation to the hapless father of the girl. Sciascia suggests that the points he makes are a guide to the Mafia's mediating skills and its use of this ability to gain financial and political clout. Don Rasconà agrees that someone should intervene to stop the stubborn baron from perpetrating an injustice against the two lovers. In a soliloquy meant to illustrate his main argument, he poses a rhetorical question: who should act as intermediary between the stubborn baron and the dejected father? The reply is self-evident. The father of the girl cannot. The law cannot. He is the only one who can. Unlike the law that brings justice only to a few, he is force, and force is everyone's law. Don Rasconà goes on to explain that when the weak, the oppressed and the betrayed found out that justice meant treachery and violence, they agreed to make violence and betrayal their justice. He goes on to say: "You call this Mafia. Actually what it is, is a revolution of the social order…since the law is unjust and a liar, I place myself above the law." Don Rasconà ends his peroration with an allusion to the coming elections emphasizing that he alone is the one who elects the new representatives to the Italian Parliament in Rome; thus his power, although invisible, is present in every aspect of Italian life.[9]

Sciascia explains that the comedy makes the following points: due to its language and its unique characteristics Sicily is one nation, the Mafia is the invisible government that operates behind the visible but ineffective government of central Italy, which in turn is often outmaneuvered by clever godfathers. If Sciascia's reasoning is followed to the end, it is easy to see why the organizing principle of the Mafia follows other sovereign governments by relying on a military procedure where personal status and degrees of authority are carefully adjudged. Yet, the Mafia is a government in itself, with its own staff and its own unequivocal judgment.

Mafioso-style behavior can be detected in certain characters of Sicilian literature. Often it is introduced in the narrative to give readers a clue to their future actions. In Giovanni Verga's 1881 book titled *The House by the Medlar Tree* or *I Malavoglia*, Toni Malavoglia back home from the Navy is shown strutting, *annacari* (the traditional walk of the Mafioso). Toni's growing dissatisfaction with the hard labor and the meager income from fishing prepares the reader for the attempted robbery. At the trial Toni, who is caught in a lava field with two companions ready to steal, will be accused of contraband and the attempted murder of Don Michele, the local customs sergeant whom he stabbed in the melee that followed the robbery. Toni will get by with a light sentence because Dr. Scipioni, a lawyer, cleverly turns his stabbing of Don Michele into an attempt to defend the family honor, compromised in this case by Don Michele's advances to Toni's youngest sister, Lia. Dr. Scipioni makes clear that Toni was determined to save the honor of the family, an understandable duty that lets Toni get by with a minimum sentence of five years in prison.

Indirect implications of Mafioso behavior can be found in the plays of Luigi Pirandello as well. In his novel *I Vecchi e i Giovani (The Old and the Young)*, Pirandello invites readers to scan the murky waters of the Sicilian political quagmire to discover the scandalous behavior of people in charge of government posts. It is useless to look for direct references to the Mafia in Pirandello's work, they are not there, still allusions are woven within the texture of the narrative and the psychology of his characters. In a way Pirandello shares *sentire mafioso* with many of his personages who are compelled to live on the fringe of society in order to come to terms with relentless human curiosity threatening their privacy. What seems paradoxical in Pirandello's characters is largely a reaction to the historical scars Sicily has sustained throughout the centuries. Law and order is seldom compatible with the welfare of the people. Centuries of foreign rule, territorial abuses, and extreme poverty rendered more poignant by feudal lords' display of opulence and the brutal repression of popular uprisings explain, even justify, Sicilian distrust of authority. Traditionally the family has been the only institution capable of resisting outside pressures. It is not surprising if the Mafia claims that the family is the chosen bond of honored friends brought together by shared interests and reciprocal protection. *La roba* and *omertà* function in perfect symbiosis.

The complexities of Sicilian culture, however, do not end here. In Sicilian tradition the drive for power and the accumulation of riches are considered a prelude of death. The Mafioso acts with the finality of someone running a race he knows he is destined to lose. Giovanni Falcone, Director of Penal Division in the Ministry of Justice, *cadavere eccellente*,[10] in his last interview with French journalist Marcelle Padovani referred to the Mafia as the "culture of death," insisting that this qualification applied not only to the Mafia, but also to everything Sicilian. He went on to say:

> "Solitude, pessimism, death are the themes of our literature from Pirandello to Sciascia. It is as if we were people who have lived too long and all of a sudden feel tired, drained, emptied, like Don Fabrizio in Tomasi di Lampedusa [*The Leopard*]. Affinities between Sicily and the Mafia are many. I surely am not the first to say so. If I do it is not to incriminate all Sicilians. On the contrary I do it to make clear what is the battle against *Cosa Nostra*. It requires not only a specialization in the subject of organized crime, but also a special interdisciplinary preparation."[11]

The interdisciplinary preparation to which Falcone refers is the understanding of typical manifestations of Sicilian life and of political intrigue difficult for an outsider to decipher. Once more Sciascia points to a likely solution to the problem as he writes:

"To face a people and catch its characteristics as if being confronted by just one person is practically impossible especially when the intention is to give an admonition… or suggest a way to govern it. It is much safer to rely on literature, on the way writers have represented her [Sicily's] life, her way of being, the constant mobility of her reality and the variety present in the characters described."[12]

Sciascia goes on to name writers who have unveiled the secrets of the Sicilian people. There are several but Verga, Pirandello, Tomasi di Lampedusa dominate his choice. What Sciascia is suggesting is that in order to find out what the Mafia is really like readers must go to Sicilian literature. It is here that they will discover the importance of Mafioso behavior that animates characters and situations as presented by Sicilian writers.

Mafia scholar Vittorio Frosini goes even further than Sciascia. He sees much of Sicilian literature as a spy on fundamental attitudes of the society it represents. Even more pointedly he calls it "a spiritual reactor that allows the reader to identify the presence of otherwise undetectable feelings of unrest, crises in need of resolution that must be understood within the context in which they appear."[13] As the Mafia informs Sicily, Sicily informs the Mafia. Thus the reader is called to be a detective, hopefully more fortunate than prosecutors in Mafia trials constantly besieged by misinformation and a wall of *omertà* impossible to crack. In spite of these drawbacks apparent from the start, the 1987 Palermo maxi-trial of 465 indicted Mafiosi delivered 342 convictions with sentences adding to a total of 2655 years in prison, not including the nineteen life terms adjudged to members of the *cupola*. It was not long, however, before business as usual resumed. As recently as August 2003 the Italian government admitted the impossibility of eliminating the Mafia from the national scene and suggested some form of *convivenza* ("cohabitation") to ease the tension and stabilize the situation which notes the ability of the Mafia's adjustments to changing social and economic conditions (a factor constantly present in Sicilian literature), mix with ordinary people without creating specific problems for the Mafiosi, rely on intimidation and violence, and be faithful to oneself regardless of the circumstances. In short, to be and to remain *la stessa cosa* ("the same thing") at all times.[14] Even if frustrated, Italians have kept their sense of humor. They call *Cosa Nostra–Casa Nostra* ("Our House").

Punning, however, does not solve the problem. In an effort to reduce Mafia activities to a minimum Law 646 the legislative edict of the Italian Republic issued September 13, 1982, asserts that the Mafia is no longer considered a mere criminal association since it has specific goals it can achieve through legal means. The legislation, mainly designed to stab Mafiosi in the pocketbook, specifies:

> "An association can be called Mafioso when the members avail themselves of intimidation, of close associative ties with each other, of obedience and *omertà* in order to commit crimes, acquire directly or indirectly the administration or the control of economic activities, of concessions, of authorizations, of public contract work and utilities in order to realize unlawful profits and [obtain] privileges for themselves and others."

Law 646 is based on testimonials and the experience of judges who often have paid with their lives for their role as Mafia prosecutors. Rocco Chinnici, who would become one of these victims on July 28, 1983, left a definition basic to the understanding of the Mafia and, as a consequence, to the formulation of the new law:

> "The Mafia has always been reactionary, conservative, always defending, and therefore, accumulating wealth. At first it was to safeguard the feud, now [to protect] large, public contracts, the richest markets, the smugglers who travel all over the world and have control over millions and billions. *Mafia then, is a tragic, relentless; cruel vocation to get rich* [italics mine]."[15]

Florentine scholar, Leopoldo Franchetti inquired into the nature of the Mafia in 1875 with the help of his friend, Sidney Sonnino, while in Sicily. Franchetti's definition is still valid today; he stated:

> "The Mafia is the union of people in different social status, of all professions, who, without apparent display, or evident

relationship, always unite to promote their reciprocal interest devoid of any consideration for law, rules or public interest. It is a medieval feeling of someone intent to provide for the care and the safety of his person and his belongings through his ability and his influence without the need to depend on the authorities and the laws."[16]

In over a century the profile of the Mafia has not changed substantially. The only noticeable progress is that Law 646 has been approved by the procrastinating Italian legislature.

The fight against Mafia power had a perceptive witness, Giuseppe Fava, who would become a victim of the Mafia in Catania, September 5, 1984. In his brief career as a playwright and journalist Fava, founder and editor of the monthly *I Siciliani*, fearlessly exposed Mafia abuses becoming a spokesman for the poor and the dejected. His campaign against the exploitation of minor members of the *onorata società* who have no option but follow orders, were important factors in determining his murder. Fava's plays are peopled with various types of humanity pleading their case in trials far too realistic to be considered sheer fiction. Fava is mainly concerned with hopeless, ignorant Sicilians who testify to the inefficiency of the government and the cowardice of powerful Mafiosi who use them only to abandon them when they no longer need their services. It is a calamity that has plagued Sicily for centuries and even today shows no sign to subside. On one side are the godfathers, skillful exploiters of human weakness, on the other useless parasites who live on the fringe of society and carry out their murders in constant fear of reprisal. The godfathers have the advantage of understanding their victims and, strange as it may seem, to empathize with them. It is not only their wealth, but the insight they have into the way Sicilians think and act, that gives them the ability to outwit legal procedures.

Fava's *La Violenza* (1969) is a drama in three acts that takes place in a Sicilian courtroom during one of the many Mafia trials predating the 1987 maxi-trial in Palermo. The play presents the case of Giacalone, an illiterate, helpless Mafioso who is accused of committing two politically motivated murders he has been ordered to carry out by the Mafia. Facing the judge, Giacalone allows that his political record is hazy. He has switched his allegiance from one party to another with no seeming reason. His ignorance of political issues is abysmal since he cannot read or write. He wonders what the judge's words have to do with his murder of two men in prison. In a candid moment he even admits that he was trying to understand which political party was most useful to his needs. "At first I thought the Monarchic, then the Communist, then the Christian Democratic Party...What was I supposed to do?"[17] Giacalone does not understand how his politics relate to the murders he has committed. Unruffled by the sudden revelation, the judge points out that in the last ten years Giacalone has been known to belong to four different parties. Giacalone explains that since WW II all parties wanted to be in charge. Since the Fascists had mysteriously disappeared at the end of the war, each party was trying to get its share of members. Giacalone asks the judge: "Excuse me, your Excellency, where have you been all this time?" Scared by his daring, he quickly adds:

> "What I mean, your Excellency, is that I have seen men like you have a change of mind from evening to morning: 'you must vote for the king Giacalone, have you lost your mind?' and a month later, 'jackass you don't even have a *lira* but you want to vote against the Communists.' I can't read or write! I was trying to understand which party was most useful to me. At first I thought the Monarchist, then the Communist, then the Christian Democratic. It seemed to be the favorite...what has this got to do with the murders anyway?"

Feeling that the questions are getting nowhere, the judge motions Giacalone back to the *gabbione* ("the cage") where other Mafia members are waiting their turn to be questioned. But he insists:

> "Do you want the real truth *Signor Procuratore*? I am nothing. I'm not protected by anyone. I have no crooked amici on my side. I am not even a crook...You can't understand what it is to be a man who has no protection, who is not even able to rebel when they kick his ass while he crosses the public square...He is worth less than a dog."

Giacalone's tirade is greeted by laughter from the cage where the other Mafiosi are waiting their turn. He knows he must leave the stand but feels a desperate urge to be heard. He appeals to the judge: "Can't you see what they are doing to me? They are capable of killing my children. If I ever get out I hope to have the courage to hide by their house and shoot them in the face, one by one…" After shouting a Mafioso's worst threat–the disfigurement of a man's *omo* ("facial features")–Giacalone turns away. As the first act ends, Giacalone sees a guard walk toward him. He backs to a bench where other prisoners are seated. Fava's stage directions read: "In the shadow all are still. Silence." *Omertà* freezes the Mafiosi in a fog of half-truths making the law's attempt to distinguish facts from lies an impossible goal.

La Violenza strikes a balance between victim and victimizer. Later in the play, a second confrontation occurs between the presiding judge and another defendant who is more important than Giacalone. A friend, a lawyer colleague, who pleads the cause of his innocent client by using a standard excuse in Mafia trials, poor health, represents Crupi, a lawyer and a powerful godfather. Crupi proves to be a reasonable man. He even agrees with the judge claiming if he were in his place he would behave with the same distrust. He admits that the dam he was supposed to build with public funds had never been built. As for the thirty thousand votes he usually got from the electorate, he was entitled to use them the way he wanted. He recognizes that the judge has every reason to believe him guilty of the twelve murders for which he has been indicted. He even admits it's entirely possible he ordered them himself. The problem for the law, however, is to find the evidence. All witnesses that could testify against him are dead.

Caught by surprise by the unexpected confession, Crupi's lawyer interjects that his client is sick. Accustomed to such tactics the judge points out that the accused party was about to make an important statement to the court. Crupi resumes his testimony. He even admits that he might have ordered two other murders. "Why not?" he interjects, "they were crooks, two sons of bitches, always cheating, stealing, cursing." He concludes by motioning toward the cage, where the other Mafiosi wait to be sentenced. "You brought me here and placed me with those men. I want to be with them to the end." The judge points out that those men he values so much are thieves and murderers. Crupi is unimpressed. *"Signor procuratore* can't you see what is going on in the outside world? Can't you see how men relate to each other? The same is happening all over. Some men are lucky, some evil, some corrupt...on the other side of the coin there are those who are defenseless, weak, stupid." As the *Procuratore* objects that according to this evaluation all murderers should go free, Crupi replies:

> "You never can tell, *Signor Procuratore.* In the outside world the powerful kill a man day by day by denying him a job, a school for his children, respect from other people, honor, happiness... they make him beg for forgiveness and pity, they make him vote for a political party he knows nothing about, for candidates he despises, they make him say *sissignore* [yes sir] and *nossignore* [no sir] on command and destroy his conscience. They even deprive him of his dignity as a man, which is worse than being dead...*Signor Procuratore*, to drive a man to such extremes is worse than killing him!"

Crupi motions toward the men locked in the cage insisting that by killing men who were their enemies they only took from them something they did not deserve—the right to be alive. At least they gave them the satisfaction of dying like men. Crupi sits down. The defense comes forth arguing that since there is no assurance that Crupi will be able to attend another session since he is not well, Luciano Salemi, brother of the murdered mayor, should be questioned now. His testimony will shed light on the moral and human stature of the indicted man. Salemi is ushered in the courtroom and shown a seat facing the judge. The Defense says "Allow me to pose my question to someone holding an opposite point of view." He turns to the bench where Crupi is seated and asks: "Defendant Crupi what is your opinion of this man?" Crupi rises slowly from the bench. "For all I know...he is a man who is not worth very much." The Defense replies, "And in your opinion, when is a man not worth very much?" Crupi answers, "When he sells out cheap." Thus the problem is not selling out, but selling out cheap. *La roba* casts its shadow on Crupi's evaluation. If the bribe does not come up to expectations then the end does not justify the means. Crupi's harsh realism is rooted in his negative opinion of human nature. Paradoxical as it may seem, his view coincides with Giacalone's, even if their perspectives are conditioned by the different place they hold in the Mafia. While Crupi gets respect because of his powerful role as godfather and his vast wealth, Giacalone is vilified by what his peers consider cowardice aggravated by poverty. Thus Giacalone is despised, Crupi respected. Yet it is Crupi who best describes Giacalone's plight by insisting with the judge that there are many ways to kill a man. In fact Crupi understands Giacalone's situation much better than the judge. He is not moved by pity, but by a clear perspective of the problem that has plagued Sicily for centuries: the poverty of the *bassa Mafia* ("low Mafia") often forced to carry out criminal practices in order to survive. This is in obvious contrast with the *alta Mafia* ("high Mafia or ruling Mafia") who are able to find a way out through highly placed connections and inscrutable alibis. It is probable that in a real life scenario Crupi would have ordered a hit on Giacalone since his presence could mean an eventual indictment for him and his associates.

Fava, a reformer with humanitarian ideals, is primarily concerned with social changes in Sicily by requesting a more equitable distribution of wealth. Targeted for his relentless accusations against the Mafia, Fava became another *cadavere eccellente* in the long list of the honorable society. Another victim of the mob, Judge Rocco Chinnici, shortly before he was killed on July 28, 1983, expressed sentiments similar to Fava:

> "The Mafia seems to have popular consensus because it gives work to thousands of people, to thousands of families. This is simply not true. It is not a consensus. To make a living wage, a person must work, so he will take work from [anyone including] the Mafia."[18]

The paradox of the Mafia, its indomitable race to accumulate *la roba*, the way it protects undercover operations through *omertà* are peculiarly symbolized by Sicily's logos, the *Trinacria*. The *Trinacria* is a grotesque arrangement of three bare legs adorned with

Mercurial wings spinning around a snake-infested head of Medusa whose wide-open eyes stare fixedly into space. Speed, accuracy, and relentless engagement seem to emanate from this mysterious symbol. By ironic coincidence the vision of constant motion and perfect stillness that are combined in the *Trinacria* seem to express Judge Giovanni Falcone's definition of the Mafia as *contropotere* ("counter power") in constant motion aiming to take over the economy of the entire country. To be entirely fair Falcone, himself a Sicilian, granted the Mafia some redeeming values such as courage, friendship, respect for tradition. These virtues, however, had been perverted by the acquisition of *la roba* and reliance on *omertà* as the means to gain access to Italian industry, commercial enterprises, and various forms of popular entertainment—certainly the cinema. The ability of communicating through silence is one of the Mafia's greatest assets. Mobster Joe Bonanno, an expert in the art, explains in his biography:

> "All men have eyes, Machiavelli says, but few have the gift of penetration. I fully realize that for an outsider the gift of penetration is a difficult one to attain when considering my world, because we of that world are normally silent, and when we do speak we use terms of an alien culture."[19]

Bonanno's description of his parting from cousin Stefano Magaddino who held him prisoner under mysterious circumstances is a telling example of the importance of eye contact in a world where words remain unspoken. "With our eyes only we said to each other: You know what I know. I know what I know. And no one else will really know as we know."[20]

The gift of penetration, so essential to mob communication can be illustrated by some of the evidence introduced by government lawyers in the 1987 Palermo maxi-trial. To demonstrate *Cosa Nostra*'s use of codes in misleading police investigators, Don Tommaso Masino Buscetta, one of the witnesses, told the following story. Two Mafiosi sharing his prison cell told him that they were caught by surprise by police officers that stopped their car. Before the agents could start a search and find the gun they had concealed in the glove compartment, they exchanged a glance reaching a silent agreement that while one knew where the gun was, the other was completely unaware of its presence. Another incident, still reported by Buscetta, dealt with the murder of Salvatore Cappiello. Members of the Partanna-Mondello family were arrested for the crime and brought to the *Ucciardone*, Palermo's prison. One of them, Salvatore Davì, greeted Buscetta with the words *nui consumammu,* Sicilian for the phrase "we are ruined." By using the plural, Salvatore signaled to Buscetta that the entire Mondello family had approved the murder he had committed.

Leonardo Sciascia in his tale "Death and the Knight" tells the story of a journalist who had sought political secrets in the trash of Henry Kissinger and compares it to the American police trying to find "the secrets of the Sicilian American Mafia in the refuse of Joe Bonanno. Although a popular slogan insists, "the garbage never lies," such was not the case with officer Ehrmann. The message he found in the garbage was "CALL TITONE WORK AND PAY SCANNATORE." Nothing could be clearer for Ehrmann; in Italian *scannare* means 'to slaughter' and a *scannatore* is 'one whose job is to slaughter.' Sciascia correctly points out the feeling of inferiority many Sicilians experience once they start comparing the island's dialect to Italian proper and suggests that for this reason the Sicilian word *scanaturi* had been italianized to *scannatore* in the Bonanno household. "The jotting was no more than a note to remind the writer to pay a Sicilian-American joiner, Titone by name, for one of those huge, meticulously planed tables of strong wood on which women knead bread, make lasagna, tagliatelle, pizza or focaccia...Scannaturi is the definition given in the year 1754, by the Jesuit Michele del Bono. Had Bonanno naively italianized the word, or had he set out to play a joke, a joke for his own benefit, on Ehrmann?"[21]

Words are indeed deceptive. Since *mezza parola* is sufficient to deliver a message, the half word chosen for the occasion must be deliberate and appropriate. Most Mafiosi are shrewd psychologists and never use a word unless they are sure to be on target. Prosecutor Giovanni Falcone explains that the use of *Signore* in front of a person's name, a sign of courtesy in Italian, is used merely to indicate someone who has no right to be named with the forms used to address important Mafia members Zio or Don, or called with the university degree they earned: doctor, lawyer, engineer. Falcone points out that *pentito* Salvatore Contorno, a witness in Palermo's first maxi-trial in 1986, addressed Michele Greco, considered even then the boss of *Cosa Nostra*, as "Il signor Michele Greco" showing by his greeting the extent of his spite. The language of Sicilian men of honor is sealed in silence. According to Falcone the reason is simple. A real Mafioso does not lie. When he can't answer questions he remains silent.

In most Sicilian literature, unless the author purposely chooses to share information with the reader, Mafioso behavior must be discovered through character motivation or through personal feelings that reveal Mafioso tendencies. Clues may emerge in the way a character speaks, in his philosophy of life, even in his obsession with death. Often conclusions can be only tentative since the parlance of the Mafia, fictional or otherwise, goes beyond the boundaries of conventional speech as Mafiosi are unwilling to take risks by expressing in words or motions information only members are called to understand. When dealing with writers as subtle as the Sicilians, the Mafioso's discretion in communication can lead to careful stylistic choices that ask the reader to decipher not what the author says but what the author means. Shortly, the writer's technique becomes similar to the Mafia's, as it demands intuition on the reader's part to detect and decode the message. As is to be expected, the challenge in selected Sicilian writers is meant only for individuals willing to go along. Other readers will be absorbed by the content but will remain unaware of Mafia machinations in the literary labyrinths of *Trinacria*. The history of Sicily seems indispensable to determine why Sicilian Mafiosi behave the way they do and even more why they still operate convinced of the right of their actions–bribery, conspiracy, murder–as they deal with a government unwilling or unable to confront the dangerous situation facing the Italian Republic. Thus the Mafia continues to prosper in a society that prefers to circumvent danger rather than face it.

The triangular shape of Sicily with its sunny, open shores is an invitation to stop and enjoy what the island has to offer. Throughout its history inhabitants of the Mediterranean basin and Europeans from the frozen lands of Scandinavia have taken up the invitation and have occupied the island. As a result, Sicilian history is a vivid reminder of occupation, poverty, futile revolutions and frustrated resignation that often broke in bloody confrontations. The beginning and development of the Sicilian saga are essential to the understanding of the Mafia. Literary works ranging from folk tales to plays, to thematic recurrences will be examined to determine the presence of Mafioso behavior in the literature of the island. Closer analysis of textual evidence will be devoted to selected works by Giovanni Verga, Luigi Pirandello, Federico De Roberto, Tomasi di Lampedusa and Leonardo Sciascia. This is skimming the surface of Sicilian writers who have cast light on the psychology and the behavior of the Mafioso. Hopefully other writers will approach the subject and show how the Mafia fills an important role in Sicilian literature.

II

Sicilian History: A Merger of Fire and Ice

Sicily is strategically located in the basin of the Mediterranean. On one side the island faces Italy and Europe, on the other Asia Minor and Greece while the coast that shapes the island into a triangle is open to the African continent. Sicilian scholar Giovanni Cucinotta claims that Italy is inconceivable without Sicily, an opinion shared by several authorities on the history of the Mediterranean.[1] Hills and mountains dominate the island of Sicily, a perimeter of 25.460 kilometers. Fourteen per cent of the flatlands in the center of the island are covered with argyle, a mixture of silicate and aluminum useful for bricks and modeling figurines but little else. Sicilian historian Antonino De Stefani points out that Sicily has generated a people of peoples. This is not a hasty opinion but an observation meant to describe Sicilians for what they are, not for what mainland Italians think they ought to be.[2] The fate of Sicilians throughout history has been to give themselves laws and develop traditions only to see them destroyed by violent conquerors that, in many instances, settled there and became part of the local population.

Sicilian myths find their roots in the Greek epic that persisted in popular tales and later merged with the stories of Charlemagne, his paladins and the importance of honor. Greek colonists settled in the southeast of the island, circa 735-725 B.C. Their influence became dominant overriding the presence of the Phoenicians (Carthaginians) who had settled in the northwest of the island. It is important to remember that the Greeks did not come as conquerors, but as settlers eventually known as *Sicelioti*. Sicily became so prosperous that it surpassed in power and wealth the Greeks' original homeland. Legend wants Daedalus, after his escape from Cnossos' labyrinth with his doomed son Icarus, to land in Sicily where his reputation as artificer and clever planner of mazes earned him a warm welcome and an invitation to stay. Greek settlers initiated the partition of large holdings of land, *latifondi*, assigned as a prize or a rental fee to proprietors who had them cultivated either by slaves or servants. Redistribution of land opened the way for litigation; as a matter of fact Sicily can claim to be the birthplace of lawsuits. It was in Sicily that Corax of Syracuse and his pupil Tisias founded what eventually became known as the Art of Rhetoric. Gorgias of Leontini (466-405 B.C.) was the best-known exponent of faultless persuasion, a skill that has never failed lawyers in the island, certainly not in recent times when powerful godfathers have relied on their grandiloquence to clear suspicions surrounding their activities.

After the Punic wars and the defeat of Carthage (260-242 B.C.) the Romans occupied the island (212-210 B.C.). Since they considered the land property of the state, they used Sicily as a granary. The inhabitants were allowed to retain 10% of the crop while 90% went to Rome. The territory was subdivided into huge *latifondi* owned by absentee landlords. The terrible conditions afflicting the local inhabitants fomented several revolts followed by bloody repressions. Octavius Augustus (emperor 27 B.C.-14 A.D.) proved more merciful than most emperors that followed, but the social and economic status of Sicily would not improve for centuries. As a result of land misdistribution and the greed of landowners, the abyss separating the very wealthy from the very poor became an evil enshrined in Sicilian society.

The fall of Rome (476 A.D.) determined the Byzantine takeover of the island. While Greek influence became once more an important factor in the island's cultural ambience, the heavy taxation imposed by the new conquerors drained the resources of the population. In 827 A.D., Arab forces led another invasion and although seventy-five years lapsed before they occupied the entire island, they proved generous enough to make Sicily an independent principate (960 A.D.) under the rule of the Kalbiti. For the first time in its history Sicily was united under one leader and experienced a period of resurgence. Palermo boasted 350,000 inhabitants and the whole island enjoyed prosperity till then unknown. The Arab conquest brought to the island an exceptional flourishing of literary studies, languages and sciences. This ideal state of things, however, did not last and the Normans, who under the leadership of Robert the Guiscard had already assured themselves a foothold in southern Italy by conquering the regions of Puglia and Calabria, decided to add Sicily to their expanding kingdom. In 1060, Roger, Robert's brother, conquered Messina and continued the invasion of the island. His son, Roger II, claimed all Norman territories and in 1130 crowned himself Rex Siciliae, king of Sicily. The rule of the Normans could be labeled enlightened Feudalism insofar as they closely watched the feudal lords but never interfered unless things got out of hand. Unique among their peers, the Normans never discriminated against the multitude of nationalities in Sicily. They also established a first never to be repeated in the history of Sicily: promotions based on merit rather than bribes. The paradoxical blending of Arab and Norman characteristics has been described as a merger of fire and ice giving the island a lasting lack of unifying characteristics that succeeded in making Sicilians at odds with each other. The consensus among historians seems to be that there is a Sicily but there are no Sicilians.[3] Norman power was followed by German rule culminating in the magnetic personality of Frederick II, king of Sicily and emperor of Germany (1124-1250). In the *Commedia* Dante sums up Frederick's role as well as the eventual end of Norman power in Sicily when in the "Heaven of the Moon" he speaks with his mother, Constance d'Hautville (1154-1198), daughter of Roger d'Hautville. Constance was the last heir of the Norman rulers in Sicily. She was forced to leave the convent and marry the emperor Henry VI (1165-1197), son of Frederick Barbarossa (Red Beard). Their son, Frederick II, was indeed *l'ultima possanza*, 'the last power', as Dante refers to him in *Paradiso* (3:120). The death of Frederick II saw the end of the Hohenstaufen dynasty and of its influence in Europe. The demise of Norman supremacy, however, did not mark the end of feudalism in Sicily. In different forms the system prevailed until the end of WW II. Giovanni Cucinotta points out a curious phenomenon that deserves more attention than it has received to date. By the time Sicily adopted the feudal policy of distributing the land to various barons (XI-XII c.), the rest of Europe had already given up this system born in the ninth century under Carolingian rule in favor of more updated forms of land management. This means Sicilian history suffered a lasting time lag that made the island out of step with the rest of Europe and subject to the phenomenon sociologist Santo Mazzarino calls "history slowed down." Still according to Mazzarino this time lag that isolated Sicily from political developments elsewhere in Europe produced historical passivity, "a static mood that psychologically became translated into a conviction of the immutability of things and of life."[4]

As the historical scenario evolves the defeat of Manfredi, son of Frederick II, by Charles d'Anjou Lord of Provence in the battle of Benevento (1226), ended Norman rule in Sicily. The French proved cruel and abusive and the government they installed was completely indifferent to the welfare of the island. The capital was transferred from Palermo to Naples, giving Sicilians another occasion for hating French rule. Oppressive fiscal policies, disregard for local traditions and constant abuse of the population made the situation intolerable. On Easter day, March 31, 1282, the rape of a bride-to-be by a French soldier sparked the incident that came down in history as *Vespri Siciliani* ("Sicilian Vespers"). As a consequence French soldiers in the island were slaughtered without mercy. The incident took hold of popular imagination and came down through the centuries. Here is godfather Joe Bonanno's version:

> "As it happened, a young lady of rare beauty, who was soon to be married, was going to church with her mother when a French soldier by the name of Droetto [italianized form for Drouet] under the pretext of helping the tax agent manhandled the young lady. Then he dragged her behind the

church and raped her. The terrified mother ran through the streets, crying "Ma fia, ma fia!" This means 'My daughter, my daughter' in Sicilian. The boyfriend of the young lady found Droetto and killed him with a knife. The mother's cry repeated by others, rang throughout Sicily. Ma fia soon became the rallying cry of the resistance which adopted the phrase as an acronym for <u>M</u>orte <u>a</u>lla <u>F</u>rancia <u>I</u>talia <u>A</u>nela."[5]

Not everyone agrees with Bonanno's version of the etymology of Mafia–reliable historians insist the cry was "mora, mora," ("die, die")–yet the explanation finds an echo in the code of honor so central to Sicilian culture and so convenient as an excuse for murder.

In spite of the patriotic sentiments evoked by the incident, Sicily's problems were far from over. Fearing the return of the French, who had left after the insurrection, the island offered the crown to Peter III of Aragon (1282) who was only too glad to accept. The last king of Aragon, Frederick III (1296-1337) tried to revive the economy by reforming the state's legislation and inaugurating a constitutional monarchy that gave Parliament an important role in decision making. Members of Parliament, however, belonged either to the aristocracy or to the clergy, two classes traditionally uninterested in improving the lot of the peasants. Unfortunately this pattern would persist in the island for over four centuries through Aragonese and Spanish domination. This period often referred to as *storia chiusa* ("closed history or stalemate") kept the island completely cut off from intellectual and political trends in the rest of Europe. The Spanish kings, sovereign rulers of Sicily, never lived on the island. They left in charge a series of cruel, incapable *Viceré* (representatives of the king), and ignorant, abusive barons callously indifferent to the needs of the people who found no respite from heavy taxation and from the loss of sequestered crops. Violent outbreaks quelled by bloody repressions kept the peasants in line. Those who survived the horrors of the backlash returned to living conditions made worse by the uprising. In 1487 the Spanish instituted the Inquisition, a move quickly followed by the expulsion of the Jews (1492) with catastrophic consequences for the economy of the island deprived of capital investments and a large share of its industries. Spanish administration gave rise to the phenomenon of

Spagnolismo, a cultural term implying corruption, haughty intolerance, bravado, ability to cheat and steal from established authority. Inevitably cynicism took over to the point that swindling the state became a skill worthy of admiration and respect. Such conditions encouraged the phenomenon of banditry that soon became a threat to travelers in the countryside. Legend wanted the outlaws to steal from the rich to give the poor. In reality, they were as greedy as the barons who used their services to keep peasants in line and collect the crops. Often the bandits relied on a *campiere*, a supervisor of the fields placed in charge by the absentee landlord to safeguard his interest. The *campiere* proved to be worse than the landlord by harassing the peasants and demanding tributes way beyond their ability to pay. Ironically, *campieri* also stole from the barons becoming increasingly bold in their demands and amassing fortunes that, in several cases, became larger than those of the landowner as Lampedusa points out in his novel *The Leopard*.

Eventually the unbearable conditions in the countryside drove the peasants to go to the cities already overpopulated and subject to the plague with dreadful regularity. As a consequence in 1575, the disease killed half of Messina's population. The problem of hunger was constant and never properly addressed. In 1647 Palermo's poor rose against the wealthy daring the clergy to follow Christ's example and feed the hungry. In a gesture of defiance a loaf of bread was placed on top of a pole and raised to the mouth of a Crucifix on the altar to make Christ a direct witness to their desperation. The meaning of this curious incident can be understood only in terms of the personalized relationship between Sicilians and mythical-religious manifestations. In Sicily, myth and Christianity still coexist. The notion of Christ does not signify a remote bond between an individual and God but represents a direct union that, on occasion, can take the form of a confrontation. The following popular song, published by Lionardo Vigo in 1857 and immediately suppressed by the authorities, makes the point:

> Un servu tempu fa, di chista piazza
> Cussi prijava a un Cristu, e cci dicia
> –Signuri u me' patruni mi strapazza
> Mi tratta comu un cani di la via;

Tuttu mi pigghia ccu la so' manazza,
La vita dici mancu hedi mia;
Si jo vi preju, chista mala razza
Distruggitila vui, Cristu, pi' mia
E tu forse chi hai ciunchi li vrazza
Oppure l'hai inchiuvati comu a mia?
Cui vole la giustizia se la fazza,
Ne speri ch'autru la fazza, pri tia
Si tu si Ôomu e non si' testa pazza,
Metti a prufittu Ôsta sentenza mia:
Jo non saria supra Ôsta cruciazza
Si avessi fatto quantu dicu a tia.
(There was once a servant in this square
Who prayed to Christ with the following words:
–Lord, my boss mistreats me
As if I was a stray dog down the road;
He steals all from me with his ugly hand
He even tells me that life is not mine
So, I pray you, this evil race
Destroy it Christ, do it in my name.
Christ replies:
And you, can't you move your arms
Or are they nailed down like mine?
He who wants justice, should carry it out
Without waiting for others to do it.
If you are man and are not a fool,
Make the most from what I'm going to say:
–I would not be hanging from this cross
If I had done what you heard me say.)

The impassionate warning of Christ exemplifies the hatred of the people against political conservatism that all along has made the Mafia a powerful exploiter of the working classes. To the Sicilians, Christ is an alter ego, an image of suffering perpetuated by someone oppressed who shares his plight since like Christ he has been betrayed and must endure martyrdom. It is a truth brought home by Salvatore Carnivale, a labor leader killed by the Mafia in 1955 for trying to introduce reforms to improve working conditions in the fields near Palermo. To a Mafioso who was trying to buy his loyalty as a friend and then threatened to kill him, he said: "come, kill me, but tell those who sent you that when they have killed me they have killed Jesus Christ."[6] While relating the capture of 'Ntoni Malavoglia and his accomplices in *I Malavoglia,* Giovanni Verga reveals his Sicilian mode of feeling by describing the powerless Ntoni caught in a criminal act as a helpless victim bound and tied like Jesus[7] evoking the ever lasting symbol of anyone persecuted by the law.

With the return of the French sent by king Louis XIV (1675) eager to defeat the Spanish, the situation hardly improved. On September 27, 1674, the Sicilians welcomed back the Spaniards proving that there is some truth in the belief that Sicily has never determined its own destiny but has been used all along as a pawn in European transactions. This became a fact in 1713 when the Treaty of Utricht awarded the island to Victor Amadeus of Savoy king of Piedmont, a very plain, unpretentious man, a far cry from the arrogant pompous Spanish grandees the Sicilians had learned to hate but also to admire for their splendid entourage. When in 1720 Victor Amadeus was offered to trade Sicily for the island of Sardinia he gladly accepted and left without regret, a feeling shared by the islanders disappointed by his lackluster performance. Once more Europe decided Sicily's destiny by assigning Sicily and Naples to Charles III of Bourbon, heir to the Spanish throne. Charles III proved to be an exception to the rule and showed an unusual interest in the Kingdom of the Two Sicilies, as the kingdom uniting Sicily and Naples became known. At the time Charles III left Naples to become king of Spain, he left as ruler his son, nine year old Ferdinand, under the tutelage of a Council of the Crown presided by Prime Minister Bernardo Tanucci who continued Charles' program of modernization. Marquis Domenico Caracciolo, appointed Viceroy of Sicily in 1781, gave remarkable impulse to the program. Caracciolo made an all out effort to reform the legislation and the economic system of the island by limiting the power of the barons and enacting reforms aimed at achieving a *dispotismo illuminato* ("enlightened despotism"), an oxymoron predictably unpopular with wealthy land owners afraid to lose their unlimited power over the land and the peasants. The Philosopher, as Caracciolo was called in Sicily, on March 27, 1782, officially closed the Tribunal of the Inquisition, a demise that did not please Sicilians captivated by the opulent displays of the *auto da fe* (burning of the infidels). In spite of Caracciolo's many reforms, or more likely because of them, the angry barons sabotaged the government so effectively that he had to leave the island. Soon after his departure, although still under Bourbon rule, Sicily was placed under English protection and gave itself a constitution that saw the abolition of the feudal system. The move determined a series of bloody confrontations with Bourbon rulers (1820, 1848, 1860) that lasted until Giuseppe Garibaldi (1807-1882) and his *Mille* ("one thousand volunteers"), landed in Quarto (1860) signaling Sicily's annexation to the kingdom of Italy. Garibaldi's occupation of Sicily and his campaign against Bourbon rule are fraught with legends and misinterpretations. A fact seldom placed in perspective is that the real heroes of the Sicilian campaign were Rosolino Pilo, Giovanni Corrao and Agostino Castello who landed in Sicily near Messina and advanced as far as Piana dei Greci. The arrival of the subversives, as they were called, was made public and the presence of Rosollno Pilo encouraged the people to fight the Bourbon troops. As for Garibaldi, a letter from Rosolino Pilo informing him that thirty thousand armed patriots were waiting near Palermo made him decide to take action. Garibaldi sailed with two ships, the Piedmont and the Lombard, along with an army of volunteers reaching the beach of Quarto where he started his legendary march leading to the unification of Italy.[8] The "One Thousand" became justly legendary. It was Rosolino Pilo, however, and his determination that made the annexation of Sicily to Italy a reality. Disappointment soon followed. The aftermath of victory resulted in continuing poverty for the masses and frustration for the patriots and intellectuals who had enthusiastically fought for Sicily's unification with the mainland.

It is undeniable that history repeats itself. Garibaldi's invasion was helped by the legitimate Mafia as it would happen in WW II when the invasion of Sicily, dubbed by Washington "Project Underworld," profited from the collaboration of Lucky Luciano then in prison, Joe Socks Lanza boss of New York's water front, Meyer Lansky also in prison, and other Mafia luminaries including Don

Calogero Vizzini, *capo dei capi* ("leader of leaders"), of *Cosa Nostra*, Mussolini's sworn enemy. Giuseppe Fava, the distinguished Sicilian journalist murdered by the Mafia in 1984, left the following account of the 1923 meeting in Rome between Don Calogero Vizzini and Mussolini in Rome's Palazzo Venezia. He does not give the source, but the story is credible enough to be quoted:

> "Mussolini received him [Don Calogero] in the *Sala del mappamondo*. It was a huge room where in a corner there was a desk next to a globe and an easy chair where he was seated. There were no other chairs. Mussolini watched this small, mysterious man dressed in black come forth without removing his hat. His new shoes squeaked at every step he took. 'Baciamo le mani' 'We kiss your hands' said Don Calogero Vizzini. 'I am the head of the Mafia; your lordship has nothing to fear from Sicily; we will make all Sicilians become fascists...We are the law!' Mussolini listened in silence, than rang a bell. A captain of the *Carabinieri* appeared. 'Arrest this man' Mussolini ordered. 'Take him immediately to a desert island. Arrest everyone in the village who lives within half kilometer from his house.'...Hundreds of *Carabinieri* and police agents loaded half of the population of Villalba including women and children in trucks, making sure that they were scattered in the small islands that form a crown around Sicily. Mussolini could not have imagined that that small elderly man...twenty years later, during a furious and bloody month of July would have opened the way to the Allies."[9]

A second version of Mussolini's reaction to the Mafia power comes from Sicilian writer Leonardo Sciascia who gives an account of Mussolini's visit to Sicily, circa 1925:

> "Mussolini, who worshipped the state, discovered that the Mafia was like another state. It seems that the revelation came to him while visiting a village near Palermo where the mayor was Mafioso. The mayor naively told him that it was not necessary to have so many *carabinieri* ("policemen")

because to protect the head of the government, the Duce of Fascist Italy, his own authority and prestige were enough. Mussolini inquired who was the mayor, what was the Mafia, and ordered a radical repression sending to Sicily prefect Cesare Mori, unquestionably a capable administrator, with unlimited power. Although the methods he used were contrary to civilized behavior...it must be admitted that 'Operation Mori' was radical and did not stop even when confronted with highly placed Mafiosi." [10]

The storming of western Sicilian shores by Allied troops on July 10, 1943, was orchestrated so well by Sicilian American mobster Lucky Luciano who cooperated with the FBI and his Mafia *amici* including Don Calogero Vizzini, that Allied troops suffered a minimum of casualties by securing the cooperation of the local population bitterly resentful for the way Mussolini's deputy, Cesare Mori, "The Iron Prefect," had expelled women and children from their homes and exiled them to the small islands surrounding Sicily. The truth was that no one in Italy really cared about what was going on in Sicily and thus the elimination of the Mafia became a cruel ploy for persecuting the local population. As soon as WW II was over, the problems of the Italian south resurfaced stronger than ever. The Mafia by then installed in key strategic roles with the help of Allied commanders who were convinced they were patriots eager to help, sought the quickest approach to power by building a financial empire, at first with the cigarette black market and later with the more lucrative traffic of heroin.

After WWII bandits returned to Sicily as well, personified this time by outlaw Salvatore Giuliano whose exploits led to the massacre of men, women and children at Portella della Ginestra near Palermo during a celebration of the *lavoratori* ("workers"), May 1, 1947. At ten fifteen in the morning as Giacomo Schiró, a shoemaker, was addressing the crowd, Giuliano and his cohorts started shooting from the top of Mount Pizzuta overlooking the field below where the crowd was gathered. By the time it was over, eleven people were dead and twenty- seven wounded. The nation was shocked and the Mafia, after using Giuliano as an ally in its post-World War II efforts to make Sicily independent from Italy, found its chance to abandon him along with the separatists' hope to rescind Sicily from Italy and join the United States of America, a hope Washington did not encourage. Rejected by the Mafia and hounded by the Italian army, Giuliano was killed by his cousin and first lieutenant, Gaspare Pisciotta, who shot him in the ear while sleeping July 5, 1950. The new Judas–as Pisciotta became known in Sicilian songs– was sent to the *Ucciardone*, Palermo's prison, where on February 9, 1954, he was poisoned with an espresso laced with strychnine. The reason was self-evident. He knew too much especially about the slaughter of Portella della Ginestra where, it was at first suspected and then confirmed, Giuliano had had the approval of the Mafia to carry out the slaughter.

The Mafia today is comfortably installed in high place government offices where men above suspicion too often are immune from effective controls. The only antidote to secret plotting is offered by the *pentiti* following the example of Don Masino Buscetta who, after the murder of Judge Giovanni Falcone, became a vengeful witness and revealed some of the most coveted secrets of *Cosa Nostra*. Does this signal the beginning of the end? Hardly, insist the most informed chroniclers of the phenomenon. Saverio Lodato, reporter for the Communist daily *L'Unita,* writes that ironically the new danger comes from the *pentiti,* over six hundred repentant, of which one hundred eighty-one qualify as Mafiosi under government protection. Judges are suspicious of these sudden contributors to Italy's peace of mind. And with good reason. Lodato cites the case of Salvatore Concemi second in criminal record only to Don Pippo Calò, boss of Porta Nuova near Palermo. According to other *pentiti,* Concemi took part in the murder of Judge Giovanni Falcone. Concemi, after repeated denials prompted by the fear of losing his status of *pentito,* decided to give a show of good will by leading several judges to the outskirts of Lugano, near the Swiss border. Here he pointed to a spot that after lengthy excavations revealed a container with over three billions Lire. Questions soon followed. Where did the money come from? Was it from a Swiss bank? Why was it hidden in that particular spot? Concemi recited the standard litany of I do not know, I do not remember. It goes without saying that along with his memory he lost his credibility both in Italy and in Switzerland.[11] His unwillingness to give away further information

Sicilian History: A Merger of Fire and Ice

to the investigators might have been a calculated effort to divert the ire of his former *amici* by giving the correct site but refusing to share more pertinent information. Saverio Lodato gives a final warning about the dangers of *Pentitismo* repentance:

> "Judges and investigators, including experts in Mafiologia [Studies in Mafia behavior], fear that the future of this war [against the Mafia] will be represented by *Pentitismo*. Unusual signs are pointing in that direction. Pierluigi Vigna, Florence's attorney general, sounded the alarm on January 21, 1994, when he stated that *Cosa Nostra* could be interested in placing *falsi pentiti* in public institutions. It is vital to remember that in Italy there are more than six hundred collaborators with the justice department. One hundred eighty-one of these are *pentiti Mafiosi* who have been admitted to the program. Many of them are difficult to manage and even more difficult to evaluate. There are some who would like to stun the investigators by using special effects.[12] These are individuals who tell stories of plots or special missions of international murder or who "shoot" big names hoping the judge will bite the hook."[13]

The conclusion seems to be that the chameleon nature of the Mafia allows it adequate resourcefulness to adapt to different circumstances with prodigious flexibility making its demise a mirage still looming in the distance.

III

The Mafia in Sicilian Literature: Beginnings

Approximately a century separates two events that marked the legitimacy of the Mafia in literary circles and its lasting hold on European imagination. An English traveler from Scotland with a bent for journalism, Patrick Brydone, in 1770 reported to his readers the existence in Sicily of what he humorously called the "honorable confraternity." His friend, the Prince of Villafranca, governor of Messina, appointed two members of the brotherly association as his escort through the island. In England, ten editions of Brydone's successful account of his travels were published under the title "A Tour through Sicily and Malta in a Series of Letters to William Beckford, Esq." In 1886, nearly a century after Brydone's report to his English readers about his unusual companions, the term Mafia made its official entry in the dictionary as the title of *Li Mafiusi di la Vicaria di Palermu*, a play that highlighted the criminal talents of men of honor in Palermo's oldest prison, the *Vicaria*.

Both events deserve special attention as they testify to the existence of the Mafia long before specific indications and documented research became available to provide details of what had been a local phenomenon for a long time. It is also valuable to see how contemporary Sicilian writers use traditional themes to emphasize the way Mafioso power continues to assert itself in local and national situations in an atmosphere of *omertà* meant to retain control of property. As we have seen, Giuseppe Fava's *La Violenza* (1969) offers an example of the author exposing current social problems, illiteracy for instance, underlying the plight of many victims of powerful men of honor. Leonardo Sciascia takes a similar approach in *I Mafiosi della Vicaria*, an update of the original play, where patriotic braggadocio gains the loyalty of the crowd and guarantees success for leaders who use political clout to increase their influence in the government and to gain greater access to power.

In his letters to William Beckford, Brydone describes Sicily's landscape and artistic sights that impress him the most along with the popular traditions of the island. Even of greater interest, however, is his account of the Mafia. He does not call it Mafia–the term did not exist at the time–but he describes the importance of honor to its members especially when they commit a murder for its sake. Brydone's adventure starts when the Prince of Villafranca, then governor of Messina, insists in providing him with the escort of two of his finest men to insure his safety and the safety of the two friends who travel with him. In one of his letters Brydone describes his highly recommended guides as two of the most callous, ruthless fellows to be found on the face of the earth. What he thought most unusual and hard to explain was that in Sicily they were feared, protected, but most of all respected.[1] Brydone is sure that in most countries men of their ilk would be stretched on the wheel or hung in chains from the prison's ceiling. He makes clear, however, that in spite of what might be their criminal record, the privileged treatment they receive from the prince of Villafranca was due to the realistic consideration that the mountainous zones of Sicily are infested by outlaws hiding inside caves and menacing the roads. Thus the prince had found the solution to his problems by placing them in his service and recognizing their importance. He had provided the men with his house's apparel, yellow and green livery richly embroidered in silver, and with arms consistent with their new position—a large sword, two pistols, a trombone (a short gun with a wide, round mouth) and plenty of ammunitions. Brydone was assured of their faithfulness and honesty, at least as far as he was concerned. In his letters back home he admits that they save him a lot of money. Since the former outlaws were feared, the villagers never ask for more than they had coming. In frequent conversations, Brydone's two escorts confess to murdering several people but in an honorable manner. Their compliance with what they think to be honorable makes a great deal of difference between them and common murderers. Brydone insists that though the guides should be considered criminals, they had always been faithful to their friends or, for that matter, to anyone to whom they had pledged their honor. In them, Brydone further explains: "there is an absurd blend of inveterate vice and virtue–if it's legitimate for me to use such expression–that rules their actions."[2] Even today Brydone's assessment remains one of the most remarkable opinions of Mafioso behavior on record.

The saga of the Mafia in literature becomes official with its debut on the Palermitan stage. It is here that the "honorable confraternity" is officially introduced with the name that eventually will become the identikit of members in the organization: Mafiusi. The action of *I Mafiusi di la Vicaria di Palermu* (1862), a comedy with farcical intents, takes place in the *Vicaria*, Palermo's oldest and most ominous prison. For the sake of accuracy, at the time the play was written Palermo's official prison was the *Ucciardone* built in 1840 to replace the aging *Vicaria*, and still in use today. *I Mafiusi* has the distinction of being the first literary work where some of the best known and still current Mafia jargon, *baccaglio*, is introduced.

Gaspare Mosca, a school teacher, and Giuseppe Rizzotto, a law student accused in 1848 of conspiracy against the Bourbon regime, share credit for what is to become the best known play in Sicilian popular theatre. *I Mafiusi di la Vicaria di Palermu* was staged for the first time in 1862 and consequently onto European and American stages with remarkable success. The title of the play is attributed to Gaspare Mosca who claims to have overheard a Palermitan shout during a confrontation: "Chi vurristi far u mafiusi cu mia?" ("What are you trying to do, behave like a Mafiusi with me?").[3] The incident indicates that the word Mafiusi was current street jargon at the time. Puns decipherable only to Sicilians characterize the speech of the inmates and add zest to the farce's peculiar brand of prison wit. *Galantuomo*, for instance, 'honest man' in Italian, in the Palermitan jargon of the time meant 'pig', thus when one of the characters, Don Leonardo, addresses *capomafia* ("head of the mafia") Gioacchino Funciazza with *"Buongiorno, galantuomo,"* ("Good morning honest man") Gioacchino, insulted by the greeting, replies *"Galantuomo! e chi haju la manu pilusa?"* ("Honest man! Is my hand covered with bristles?"). *I Mafiusi di la Vicaria* endows the vocabulary of the Mafia with a terminology used even today by the Sicilian and American mob such as *pagari la lampa e lu pizzu* meaning 'to pay the lamp and the beak.' While the first term presents no specific problem of interpretation, as the lamp was necessary to see at night in the dangerous darkness of the prison, the second puns on the beak-shaped end of a twirling wooden top boys used to spin in the streets of Palermo to test their skill. The *lampa* and the *pizzu* respectively indicate the initiation fee and the dues newcomers pay to the prison Mafia to gain and retain respect among the inmates—in short, it is survival insurance. *Lu pizzu* still indicates the share mob members must pay the family in business deals, more commonly however, *vagnari lu pizzu* 'to wet the beak' means to give someone a bribe.

It seems that Gaspare Mosca conceived the play after meeting Gioacchino d'Angelo, a former convict who gave him tips on prison life. According to testimonials of the time, Mosca became a member of Rizzotto's company and, for reasons unknown, the actors found a friendly welcome in *Iachinu Funciazza*'s tavern whose nickname *nciuria* ("injury") was because of the odd shape of his lips. The Mafioso tavern-keeper gave Mosca all the necessary information, more important however; he clued him to the meaning of *baccaglio*, the jargon used by criminals. Along the way Iachinu expressed a genuine admiration for statesman Francesco Crispi[4] who seems to have been introduced in the play under the pseudonym Incognito. The Marquis of Rudinì, upset by the inevitable conclusion that the prisoners were running the prison, urged Rizzotto to add a third act to the original two and have a repentant Iachinu Funciazza declare he had abandoned the *onorata società* and joined the Workers Society of Mutual Aid where he was accepted thanks to the intercession of the mysterious Incognito. Needless to say, the conversion sounds contrived. Iachinu Funciazza is far more convincing, and surely more fun, when he uses his wits to claim *lu pizzu* from his victims and to manipulate *la roba* to his advantage.

The play, written in Sicilian dialect, relies on rapid word exchanges and on the improvisation techniques typical of the *Commedia dell'arte*.[5] Among the conniving Mafiosi, Iachinu Funciazza stands out as the factotum who asks for bribes and delivers justice. The farcical elements in the play, the constant plotting to eliminate undesirable characters among the prisoners lead to the murder of an inmate, Don Nunzio-O'Cavaliere, victim as Iachinu succinctly puts it, of having failed to pay someone what he owed. Even the jailer is on the side of the murderers as he explains: "he [Don Nunzio] has confessed of having been a spy, a slanderer and having stolen this very day seven scudi [currency of the time] and a pair of pants from Don Leonardo." As the inmates are on their way to a banquet purchased with extortion money, a bell tolls. Iachinu proclaims: "The viaticum!" (all kneel and take off their caps). As the sacrament of the dead goes by he adds a philosophical afterthought followed by an appropriate quotation from Our Father: "Some cry, some laugh. God forgive us our sins as we forgive those who sin against us." The pious conclusion may have been prompted by the knowledge that none other had perpetrated the theft than himself, Iachinu Funciazza, *capo mafia* ("head of Mafia"), prison legislator and absolute boss of *I Mafiusi di la Vicaria*.

The encounter between the Incognito and the two Mafiosi, Turiddu Masticusu and Iachinu Funciazza, offers a rare insight into the way the *lampa* and the *pizzu* became operational. The following conversation takes place in the last scene of act one. The speakers are Turiddu Masticusu and the Incognito followed by Iachinu Funciazza who takes over when Turiddu fails to achieve the desired results.

TURIDDU. We kiss your hand.
INCOGNITO. Hello.
TURIDDU. Your lordship. Are you the one they have taken to cell number 14?
INCOGNITO. Yes.
TURIDDU. You must be uncomfortable. There is no air.
INCOGNITO. I found it out.

TURIDDU. No problem. I'll have them change your cell. I'll have them give you cell number 9. It's better.
INCOGNITO. Much obliged.
TURIDDU. Tell me something. Has your lordship ever been here before?
INCOGNITO. It's my first time.
TURIDDU. I'm sorry.
INCOGNITO. Thanks a lot.
TURIDDU. What I mean is: you don't know the rules of the prison.
INCOGNITO. What rules?
TURIDDU. Your lordship must pay sixty pieces for lu pizzu.
INCOGNITO. What pizzu?
TURIDDU. For the lampa.
INCOGNITO. What lampa what pizzu are you talking about? I don't understand you–that is, I don't want to understand you.
TURIDDU. You don't understand me? I am going to make you understand me right now. [*He raises his hand ready to strike him*]
IACHINU. [*Stops Turridu*] You big bastard. We are just talking, there is no hurry. [*To the Incognito*] I kiss your hand.
INCOGNITO. Greetings [*keeps reading the paper*]
IACHINU. Your lordship must understand. I must speak with your lordship.
INCOGNITO. Speak. I am listening.
IACHINU. Your lordship... will you do me a favor? Will you put down that inkwell [6] you hold in your hand?
INCOGNITO. What inkwell, this? [*he shows him the newspaper*]
INCOGNITO. [*Folding it*] I'm all yours.
IACHINU. Your lordship must know that I take care of my business with calm, without getting heated because heat is bad for the entrails. Inside this place there is a custom, a tradition, custom and tradition become law. For those who are fortunate enough to be here....there is a small fee to pay for the francisi.

INCOGNITO. What are they, French?
IACHINU. That's the name we give them. They are those who are in need. If you give us a small amount, they keep quiet–you live quietly, everybody is quiet.
INCOGNITO. Listen to me... [*he speaks in his ear*]
IACHINU. Your lordship must forgive me. I did not know, otherwise I would have paid my respects. To hell with the Cavaliere (another inmate) who has placed me in this situation. From now on you'll have the lasting respect of Iachinu Funciazza.
INCOGNITO. Let's not talk about this anymore. It's of noconsequence.[7]

The Incognito's political stature and his influence in the affairs of the island spare him the obligation of the *lampa* and the *pizzu* and gains him the services of Iachinu who is fully aware that his own interest will be better served by insuring the good will of the illustrious guest. Once out of prison, the Incognito will remember Iachinu's good will and retain him as a useful *amico*. The friendship of such highly placed politician may even have been worth a stay in prison. Iachinu Funciazza will enjoy all the protection he needs to carry out his schemes with renewed patriotic fervor. This is where Leonardo Sciascia picks him up in his updating of *I Mafiusi di la Vicaria* presented in 1966 in Milan's *Teatro Piccolo* and Catania's *Teatro Stabile*.

The updated version is simply called *I Mafiosi*. The play has greater political impact than the original largely because of a conscious effort to satirize the timeless rhetoric of powerful candidates eager to play on the audience's patriotic feelings to score political gains and to increase their hold on *la roba*. Sciascia's skill in weaving current Mafia themes with the original material offers exceptional insights into the Mafia's lasting appeal to the chauvinistic instincts of the crowd. The Mafiosi's political savvy emerges untarnished and rooted in the tradition that allows its members to act as lawful, patriotic citizens eager to serve the Sicilian people in Rome's *Montecitorio*, Italy's Parliament. In Sciascia's version of the play former convict Gioacchino Funciazza has achieved political clout to ensure a future of substantial gains through his alliance with the

Incognito, the powerful friend of his prison days. The role of the Incognito was expanded to reveal a clever politician who skillfully uses Mafioso tactics to define and protect his mission as champion of the people.

In the forward to the play Sciascia explains that he uses the Rizzotto and Mosca script merely as a guideline to retain the original description of life in prison and the names of the convicts. His goal is to update the progress of the Mafia from the time of the Bourbons and Garibaldi (1860-61) to more contemporary developments keeping the background and the historical circumstances intact.[8] The play opens with the Incognito looking for Gioacchino Funciazza. Pasquale, a neighbor, informs him that Gioacchino is again in prison for placing "a tiny button hole" in the stomach of Gennarino the butcher. Allegedly, the butcher has made a pass at Gioacchino's wife and honor becomes the excuse for murder. Pasquale philosophizes that "a man must be a man" although he admits Gioacchino could have waited for the revolution to carry out his vendetta. The action moves inside the *Vicaria* where the convicts are variously employed making brooms and kitchen utensils. In a lively exchange between Gioacchino and Minicu, another inmate, an uninterrupted flow of barbs leads to the basic rule of the Mafia: the obligation of the inmates to pay *lampa* and *pizzu* to earn the right to be left alone. Gioacchino explains to Minicu that if the lamp goes off something can happen while you are sleeping. He makes clear that the *lampa* stands for friendship, a feeling that goes along with the privilege of sleeping in peace. The play keeps following the original Mafiusi as Gioacchino threatens the Incognito with regrettable consequences if he does not pay his dues. The purpose of the fee, Gioacchino explains, is to provide a little banquet for the boys and to finance the care of indigent members of the group. Far from being impressed by the threat, the Incognito whispers his identity in the ear of Gioacchino who implores forgiveness and from then on becomes the devoted servant of his new *amico*.

Don Leonardo Vacirca a satirical portrait of the gullible intellectual, while speaking with Don Nunzio, another inmate designated by Gioacchino to be his next victim, laments that a thief has stolen his money. Leonardo expresses gratitude to Gioacchino who is trying to recuperate his stolen property out of the goodness of his heart. Don Nunzio tries to tell Leonardo that the thief is Gioacchino himself, information that takes Leonardo completely by surprise. During his conversation with Leonardo, Don Nunzio complains about feeling dizzy. The sudden ailment becomes an invaluable tool in the hands of the Mafiosi eager to do away with the man they consider a spy. Gioacchino charges two of his *amici*, Turi and Minicu, to assist Don Nunzio who has gone to get some fresh air on top of the fortress. He explains that it could be dangerous for him to be left alone since the wall embracing the bastion presents a danger for anyone susceptible to spells. Somebody should be close to him to avoid an accident. Turi and Minicu join Don Nunzio and push him over the wall making his dizzy spells end forever.

Alone with Don Leonardo the Incognito praises Gioacchino for his natural goodness, generosity, courage, intelligence and common sense. Don Leonardo objects that unfortunately Gioacchino understands only the meaning of brute force and always speaks of *morti ammazzati* ("murdered dead") as if killing people is a game. At this point Sciascia has the Incognito defend Gioacchino's behavior by making him express the Mafioso's traditional views as documented long before by English traveler Brydone:

> "In spite of this, you'll find in Gioacchino and his friends a spark...of legal knowledge, a longing for justice...in effect because of the vacuum created by a lack of legislation and the void created by our ineffective government, they have established a primitive, bloody law of their own."

The thump of Don Nunzio's body followed by terrified screams proclaims the obvious. The body of Don Nunzio is paraded on stage carried by the inmates and preceded by a priest. Elated by the success of the mission, Gioacchino invites all present to a banquet. Don Leonardo objects that eating may not be the best way to commemorate the recent death of a man. The Incognito, however, reminds him that the Greeks celebrated death with a banquet in honor of the deceased. Eager to alleviate Don Leonardo's scruples he adds: "Can't you tell how the soul of ancient Greece is alive in them?" Such irrefutable argument convinces Don Leonardo to accept the invitation. Both men join the party financed by dues paid by inmates eager to deserve the protection of the *lampa* and the *pizzu*.

The second act takes place by the house where Gioacchino lives with his wife Carmela. It is election day and following a well established tradition eligible voters wine and dine all night to assure their support for the Incognito who is well positioned to become Sicily's representative in the Italian Parliament. By now Gioacchino enjoys the friendship of His Excellency who trusts him with delicate missions he carries out with admirable success. His neighbor Pasquale is eager to become a member of the Society–the Mafia is intended here–but Gioacchino discourages his efforts by insisting that the Society existed only before the revolution:

> "It existed because we were outsiders...now we are insiders. Where is the need for a Society among us? All of us are a Society–you, me, his Excellency, the president of the bank, the judge, the guard."

But Pasquale is not a fool. He knows the Society is still there, in a different guise perhaps, but still there. Gioacchino is furious, but Pasquale, while admitting his lack of criminal credentials, insists that if necessary he can handle a knife with the best of them. "It's useless for you to deny the existence of the Society. I know it exists." He quickly exits the stage while ducking Gioacchino's boot.

The arrival of Don Leonardo, author of articles promoting the election of the Incognito, causes a stir. The Incognito's rival for Parliamentary seat, named Duina, has accused His Excellency of striking an alliance with the Mafia to secure the election. He is gone so far as to suggest that a Mafioso at the service of the Incognito had murdered the organizer of his electoral committee. Gioacchino insists that the night Duina's collaborator was shot, those accused of being involved in the murder had stopped at the home of His Excellency and had not left till after midnight. After some difficulty in recalling their whereabouts on the night of the murder, all the present agree that the overwhelming hospitality of His Excellency had convinced them to stay beyond midnight.

The play ends with the Incognito giving a rousing electoral speech. The Voice [sic] of someone in the crowd casts a sinister light on the proceedings by demanding to hear what Gioacchino Funciazza has to say. Urged by the Incognito, Gioacchino stumbles into a speech declaring him honored by the trust of His Excellency and the friendship of the people. He even declares him to be "a friend of friends." He winds up his oratorical debut with a cautionary remark. In case someone is not ready to live in peace with him, he is ready and capable to take on the challenge. The Voice promptly shouts: "Don't we know it." Turi and Minicu, Gioacchino's accomplices, grab the Voice and drag him away. The Incognito turns the incident to his advantage, praising the citizens of Palermo for their proud, generous, intelligent judgment. He then addresses the Voice who has insulted him by calling him Mafioso and accuses him of having debased the electoral contest by bringing it into the battlefield of the Mafia. In a polemic mood he poses a philological question:

> "But then, my friends, what is the real meaning of Mafia? For me and for you Mafia means elegance, pride, chivalry, sense of honor, superiority and perfection...this is the Mafia the way the Sicilian people understand it."

"What if it is the other way around?" the Voice shouts from the back. This time he is grabbed and dragged away by the angry crowd. The Incognito winds up his speech as if completely unaware of the interruption. He goes on to say that if the meaning of Mafia is what he had stated before he was interrupted, he is proud to call himself Mafioso and carry to the Parliament of a united, free, great Italy, the vivifying breath of the Mafia from their glorious island. The play ends with His Excellency waving his hands to the applauding crowd as the band strikes up "The Hymn of Garibaldi."

Sciascia's adaptation of *I Mafiosi* underscores the unscrupulous political activities of the *onorata società*. His ability to weave current Mafia tactics within the traditional framework of the play invites a thoughtful comparison with the original. The similarity of the situation, the chicanery of the prisoners, their leaders' clever use of Mafioso propaganda to manipulate the crowd allows the Society to become representative of the popular will eager to ignore the Italian government, too often insensitive to the needs of the island.

Latent hostilities between Palermo and Rome often remain unaddressed feeding the mutual distrust. It is interesting to see how in the updating of *I Mafiusi di la Vicaria di Palermu* Sciascia makes the Incognito succeed in creating convincing alibis meant to further his political aims. It is Gioacchino Funciazza, however, that emerges as the Machiavellian in the play. Gioacchino goes as far as to deny the existence of the *onorata società* simply named *società* before political alternatives. The Incognito's dependence on Gioacchino's services is Gioacchino's best assurance for a promising future. A powerful friend in the Italian Parliament will guarantee respect for him and his *amici* and doubtlessly insure a larger share of *la roba* and make their jealously kept *omertà* worthwhile.

IV

Lust, Vengeance and Honor

The importance of property and the role played by the conspiracy of silence find their way in traditional Sicilian tales narrated to this day by a *cantarinu* ("a popular singer"). *La Baronessa di Carini*, a sixteenth century tragic romance, is one of the most dramatic tales in the repertoire. Here the importance of ownership goes beyond the role of honor as adultery becomes a panacea for a husband who refuses to acknowledge his impotence and gives his silent assent to an affair between his wife and a friend, in order to claim his rights to the family property for himself and his eventual heirs. Confronted by relatives and the clergy he can no longer deny his way of compensating for his sexual problem. He opts for a bloody solution in order to rescue his honor and the honor of the family.

Italo Calvino has transcribed the next folk tale, *L'arte di Franceschiello*, from the original Sicilian.[1] The story narrates the peculiar ties between a clever godson and his *padrino* a priest eager to test Franceschiello's exceptional skill for stealing, anxious to profit from his godson's undeniable talent. Franceschiello's versatility in the art of deception follows Luigi Capuana's *Comparatico* (1882), an important story that fully understands the awesome implications that go along with the name of godfather. Giovanni Verga's *Cavalleria*

Rusticana (1884), mostly known because of Pietro Mascagni's homonymous opera (1889), explores the fatal obligation of honor. The tragic, inevitable consequences of a changing social order is the central theme of Verga's masterpieces of Italian *Verismo* ("Realism"), *I Malavoglia* (1881), and *Mastro Don Gesualdo* (1889) where poverty, ill fortune and consuming greed doom the protagonists caught in a vise of unresolved conflicts.

The period of transition preceding the installation of the Mafia in political and administrative roles traditionally reserved for members of the ruling aristocracy is examined in detail by Sicilian novelists ranging from Federico De Roberto in *I Vicerè* ("The Viceroys") (1894), to Luigi Pirandello in his 1913 little known novel *I vecchi e i giovani* ("The Old and the Young"). Forty-five years later in 1958, Giuseppe di Lampedusa's *Il Gattopardo* ("The Leopard") would cast an ironic look on the greedy, opportunistic nouveaux riches, former servants of a privileged class, as they replaced a decadent aristocracy. As history unfolds and the Mafia establishes itself in city life and increases its participation in the politics of the island, a greater number of Sicilian writers focus on these historical events and social changes. As we have seen Giovanni Cesareo's play *La Mafia* was brought to the attention of the public by Leonardo Sciascia who found it one of the best illustrations of the Mafia's ability to tighten its deadly grip on its victims.

The most powerful voice in contemporary Sicilian literature exposing the political and moral dangers of *omertà* unquestionably belongs to Leonardo Sciascia. In *The Day of the Owl* (1961), *The Context* (1971), just to mention two of his best-known works available in English translation, Sciascia reveals a passionate nature subtly restrained by sarcasm, as he relentlessly exposes the dangers of Mafia power. In *A Straightforward Tale*, the title of a novella he wrote shortly before his death, he satirizes the ability of the Mafia to circumvent truth. Tales may be straightforward, Sciascia argues, the Mafia never is. In life as in fiction the twisted plot of a darkly spun tale keeps the public guessing and the police mystified unless, as it often happens, the police are part of the plot. Sciascia's intriguing tales update Mafia operations by placing godfathers under the protection of powerful government officials involved in a conspiracy of power aimed to make *Cosa Nostra* a lasting presence in the Italian quagmire.

The above selections are a partial representation of Mafioso behavior in Sicilian literature. The tales, the plays and the novels examined here are a sampler of how the Mafia, far from being merely a criminal association, reveals itself in Sicilian life. All selections are related to the island's traditions and to its people's reliance on the code of honor, a hard to define blend of bravery, roguery and destructive behavior as reported in 1770 by Patrick Brydone and recently described in the realistic characters of Leonardo Sciascia. Priority must go to two stories, favorites in Sicilian popular tradition, *La baronessa di Carini* ("The Baroness of Carini") and *L'arte di Franceschiello* ("The Trade of Franceschiello").

The Baroness of Carini, a tale from Sicilian history dramatized by the Teatro dei Pupi, Palermo's puppet theater, is the tragic story of Laura di Trabia, Baroness of Carini (1529-1563) a woman of exceptional beauty, sensuality, and remarkable courage in facing death by the hand of her father or her husband, according to different sources. The identity of the executioner is still debated among Sicilian scholars mostly because the many versions of the murder have been transfigured by popular imagination casting a shadow on the conflict for property that, in all probability, was the real cause of the tragedy. The motive for the murder may be what distinguishes the death of the Baroness of Carini from the many Medieval and Renaissance tales of wives murdered by an outraged father or a betrayed husband. The story takes place near Palermo, in the castle of Carini built between 1075 and 1090 during Norman rule, but completed in the 16th century under Spanish sovereignty. Laura Lanza, daughter of Baron Lanza of Trabia, was born in the village of Trabia on the Palermitan coast in 1529. She was well educated. It was in the home of her music teacher that she met the two youths who became pivotal to her destiny: her future husband, Vincenzo II La Grua, son of Baron La Grua, and Ludovico Vernagallo scion of a family immensely rich but without an hereditary title. Predictably Laura fell in love with Ludovico but her family stipulated a nuptial contract with the powerful La Grua family and the wedding between Laura and Vincenzo was celebrated. Ludovico disappeared from the scene only to return to Carini years later more handsome than ever making the beautiful, childless Laura long for his attentions. A side effect of the relationship was a pregnancy welcomed by all parties since in seven years of marriage there had been no heir in sight. The birth of a girl, Caterina, was followed by an extraordinary awakening of fertility that made Laura the mother of eight children. Was Vincenzo La Grua aware that his wife's pregnancies were not due to his virility but to Ludovico's sexual prowess? Father Vincenzo Badalamenti, a local author who did extensive research on the subject, in *Carini nell'arte* ("Carini in Art"),[2] found evidence that a second marriage contracted by Vincenzo to another woman, Ninfa Ruiz, eighteen months after the murder of Laura di Trabia, failed to produce offspring. It does not seem to be out of the question that Vincenzo was well aware of his sterility and welcomed the help of Ludovico at least until the affair became public knowledge and Vincenzo, faking shock at being *cornuto* ("cuckold") had no choice but act the part of the outraged husband. The sight of the murder–Carini or Palermo?–and the executor of the deed have caused lasting disagreement among Sicilians all claiming to have the correct version of the demise of the Baroness carried out either by her father, as a 17th century ballad relates, or by her husband, as Father Badalamenti's research implies. Once the lovers had been killed, the children of Laura and Ludovico were declared bastards and disinherited. Ironically, since there were no heirs from Vincenzo's second marriage to Ninfa Ruiz, the problem of the inheritance, the coveted *roba*, remained unsolved.

Even today *La barunissa di Carini* remains one of Sicily's most popular ballads. The opening stanza, unquestionably the most famous, expresses the mourning for her death:

> Chianci Palermu, chianci Siracusa
> Carini c'e` lu luttu ad ogni casa…
> cu' la purtau sta nova dulurusa
> mai paci possa aviri a la so' casa…
> aju la menti mia tantu confusa…
> lu cori abbunna…lu sangu stravasa.
> Vurria 'na canzunedda rispittusa,
> chiancissi la culonna a la me casa;

la megghiu stidda che rideva in celu,
anima senza cappotto e senza velu;
la megghiu stidda di li Serafini
povira Barunissi di Carini!
(Cries Palermo, Siracusa cries
there is mourning all over Carini.
The one who brought these sorrowful news
may never find peace in his own home.
I have so much confusion in my mind
the heart is bursting…the blood is overflowing.
I wish that a song full of respect
would cry for the one who kept my house upright,
the most beautiful star in the sky
a soul naked, without a veil
the brightest star among the Serafini—
poor Barunissa di Carini!)

Far from being a story of romantic love and marital vengeance, *La Barunissa di Carini* can be seen as a case of *omertà* practiced by the betrayed husband till his silence about Laura's sexual indiscretions becomes inconvenient and he is forced, under pressure brought on by relatives and the clergy, to act the part of the outraged husband and vindicate his honor. Possession of land and money validated by Carolingian tradition and by Spanish rule made the wife a pawn meant to increase property for her husband through dowry and reproduction. It is an instance where honor becomes nothing more than a pragmatic routine to keep and increase *la roba* while *omertà* is merely a convenient tool that enables the scheme to succeed.

Going from a tragic event in history to fairy tales, it should be noted that in marked contrast with tales of northern Europe, Sicilian stories are exceptionally realistic. Many are concerned with survival thus they often deal with the ability of poor families to put food on the table. *L'arte di Franceschiello* ("The Trade of Little Francis")[3] is a story well known in many parts of Italy and adapted with local variations in other parts of Europe, unquestionably Sicilian, however, in implication and language since the *arte unuratamende* ("honorable trade") of the *abigeato* ("the theft of sheep") by *briganti* ("a rogue") and rural Mafiosi, is given a prominent role.

Franceschiello's negative reaction to his widowed mother's insistence that he must learn a trade shows a premature talent for disregarding ways of earning an honest wage barely sufficient to survive. Although just a boy, Franceschiello has the self-assurance and the bravado of a promising *picciottu*. To please his mother, three times he becomes an apprentice to a tradesman and three times he quits. Having reached the end of her wits and her money, the mother agrees to give Franceschiello the ten ducats she has left and to let him look for an art suitable to his talents. In various meetings with *briganti*, Franceschiello learns *l'arte onorata*, the honorable art of stealing by outwitting everyone who stands in his way. Once back home his mother, astonished by the loot he brings back, asks him what is the art he has learned. Franceschiello replies that his trade is eating, drinking and taking a walk. Not quite convinced by his profession, the mother decides to go see the boy's godfather, the local *arciprete* and tell him the art his godson has learned. The *arciprete* ("head priest"),[4] whose intuition is sharper than the mother's, tells her to send him the boy. When Franceschiello arrives he makes him a proposition he can't possibly refuse: "I have twelve shepherds and twelve dogs. If you can steal a castrated sheep from the fold, I'll give you one hundred ducats." Franceschiello dresses like a monk and goes to find the shepherds. Reassured by his disguise, the shepherds tie up the dogs and invite him to rest by the fire. Franceschiello takes a loaf of bread and a flask of wine from his beggar's sack and begins to eat making only the motion of drinking since the wine is spiked. The shepherds feel insulted by his selfishness and Franceschiello, cheerfully apologetic, passes the flask around. No sooner have they drunk than they fall asleep. Franceschiello finds the plumpest sheep, butchers and roasts it and sends a leg to the *padrino*. The priest understands that the message is from his godson who wants to make sure he knows who is responsible for the theft. Franceschiello gets his hundred ducats. The *arciprete*, however, feels the need to further confirm his godson's talents. This time he increases the bet to two hundred ducats. The goal is to take something, anything, from a small church under the priest's jurisdiction guarded day and night by a homeless pilgrim. With eight days to complete the mission, Franceschiello waits for the eighth night when the pilgrim dead tired after watching for seven days and seven nights, decides to go out to relieve himself and, back in church, to get some sleep. He falls asleep in the middle of the church giving Franceschiello the opportunity to surround him with all the statues of saints he can carry, he dons priestly robes, and goes to the altar to shout with all his power that the time for repentance has come. The terrified pilgrim asks his holiness what can he do to save his soul. Franceschiello instructs him to jump into the sack he hands him,[5] advice the pilgrim follows without questioning. Impressed by the skill of his godson, the *arciprete* pays him the two hundred ducats thinking that in order to avoid ending "inside a sack" himself, he needs to secure the friendship of the youth, an aspiring man of honor already proficient in the *arte unuratamente* ("the honorable art of stealing").

Although the story is reminiscent of the tradition of the French fabliaux popular in the 12th and 13th centuries, the language and atmosphere in this version of rural Mafioso aspirations are tied to Sicilian culture and, in this case, to the dishonest manipulations of those who should be keepers of public morality. The ability to make wealth a goal in itself coupled with the pragmatic economic reality, are the prime purposes of Mafioso behavior and an accepted way to command respect. Involvement of the clergy in the *onorata società* is a Sicilian reality declining today because of stricter supervision from the Vatican, but this is not to say that it has completely disappeared. Sure of his rights and shielded by religious privileges, Franceschiello's *padrino* is well positioned to profit from his place in the community. He can only admire, and perhaps fear, someone who shows signs of being cleverer than he is, thus he offers Franceschiello *lu pizzu*, a cut of the eventual profits even before a partnership is struck. Franceschiello's ingenuity and his ability to deceive are his best guarantee of success. As Sciascia points out in *Le Parrochie di Regalpetra* the art of stealing sheep persisted in Sicily as a means of earning extra cash till after World War II.[6] He narrates an instance where Avvocato Cravotta, a lawyer of his acquaintance, had been robbed of his sheep. It seems that the lawyer told his sorry story to someone in town. The man suggested that he should get in touch with Gaspare Lo Pinto, an influential citizen. Cravotta protested he had already denounced the robbery to the Carabinieri, at any rate he had seen Gaspare Lo Pinto, a friend of his, and had informed him of the theft but Gaspare had had nothing to say. His listener became impatient. He abruptly asked the approximate value of the sheep, and then he suggested that Cravotta should go to see Gaspare and tell him he would be willing to pay a given sum for the return of the sheep. He was ready to bet that the sheep would come home. Cravotta was amazed at the suggestion. After all, Gaspare Lo Pinto was the mayor of the town. The man giving him the advice agreed. This was exactly why he could carry out the deal without problems. Sciascia does not give the conclusion of the incident but it can be assumed the results were positive. It is the Mafia's pragmatic attitude–business first–and its ability to deal from a vantage point that enables it to operate without risking its secrecy. Survival implies to learn how to play the game and to cave in if and when necessary.

Luigi Capuana's "Comparatico" [7] is a chilling reminder of the meaning godfather holds in Sicilian tradition and the dreadful consequences for breaking the rules. Trust carried to an absurd level followed by a savage *vendetta trasversale* ("vengeance across the line") makes the legacy of "The Bond of San Giovanni," (*sic* in the English translation) powerfully clear. The traditional relationship between godfather and godson goes beyond immediate family ties to become a sacred thrust between two parties bound by a pact that demands absolute, reciprocal trust. It is difficult for someone who is not Sicilian or at least southern Italian to understand fully the meaning of *padrino*, godfather, his responsibility toward the godchild and, conversely, how the family of the godchild is obliged to give him the respect and friendship owed to someone who enjoys absolute moral authority within the boundaries of the relationship. In the introduction to the English version of the story, Alfred Alexander, noting that the title of the story needs an explanation, writes:

> "Compare means literally 'co-father,' a term originally used for two relationships: the compare d'anello or 'ring co-father' i.e. the marriage witness who signs the church register, and the compare di battesimo or 'baptismal co-father', the child's godfather in his relationship to the father (though not in his relationship to his godchild, to whom he is *padrino*

or godfather). The English language has no equivalent for this relationship between father and godfather...Eventually the term compare became a general mode of address vaguely indicating respect and approbation...In Capuana's story, the term comparatico is used in its original meaning. 'Godfathership' is a holy bound, protected by St. John the Baptist himself...and must not be violated." [8]

As Leonardo Sciascia explains, the Mafia has often used adultery as a convenient excuse for murder. *Comparatico*, the title of Capuana's story, conveys an ironical warning and makes the reader aware of the unique relationship central to the story and the dreadful consequences implied in breaking the sacred trust connatural to the role of *padrino*.

Janu Pedi, a modest but self-sufficient farmer, is approached by his neighbor Zi' (Uncle) Peppe Cipolletta who informs him that his wife Filomena and his child's godfather Pietro are having an affair. Janu thinks that his own father, who does not like his wife, has started the rumor and refuses to believe Zi' Peppe. Nevertheless his faith in his wife and the *padrino* is shaken and his generosity toward the godfather who, as tradition allows, practically lives at his house, aggravates the situation and only serves as further proof of the unholy bond. A fight with Filomena who curses Janu's father who has never liked her exacerbates the situation. At the point of death the old man confirms Ianu's worst suspicions: "you ought to know–that whore–carries on with Godfather Pietro." The revelation confirms Janu's suspicion and while working in the field, tortured by his small son's innocent display of affection for Godfather Pietro, kills him hitting him with a hoe. Once back home, he finds the excuse that the child begged him to spend the night in the country with the children of his aunt Lena. After an abundant meal and some heavy drinking as the time to sleep nears, a heavy rainstorm makes Janu invite Pietro to spend the night with them, in their bed. "Where else is there for Godfather Pietro to go? Does he really want to be carried away by the flood? We'll place her (sic) between the two of us. Can't we trust our brother in St. John?" What seems simplicity of mind arguably even stupidity, is a sarcastic anticipation of a vendetta. The woman placed in the wedding bed between the two men who have possessed her is stabbed to death along with her lover creating a symbiosis of betrayal and retribution. A truly Sicilian touch ends the story. Confronted with the murders "people thronged the streets everyone in sympathy with Janu, that poor fellow who had done the right thing and couldn't possibly be condemned by any court of justice."

A relative of the dead man seeing Janu go by handcuffed, his head erect, and a smile on his face, shouts: "so you've just begun to feel your horns after four years." Unruffled, Janu replies: "sooner than you anyway! You haven't noticed yours yet—your sister is carrying on with the baker!" [9] Traditionally the *cornuto* is reviled and denied acceptance by the community. Janu had no choice. The sympathetic reaction of the crowd must be seen in the light of the tradition of the code of honor, a tradition the Mafia has used all along to its advantage. As for inflicting a punishment fitting the crime, the Mafia is well known for the impeccable precision of its penalties. A victim's penis is amputated and placed in the mouth of the culprit to show that the former Mafioso came short to the expectations of *omo* ("a man"), by betraying the pledge of silence.

Two examples of relentless efforts to amass and retain *la roba* are two consecutive novels by Giovanni Verga, *I Malavoglia* (1881) translated into English as *The House by the Medlar Tree,* and *Mastro Don Gesualdo* (1889). The struggle of Padron 'Ntoni Malavoglia to save the family's home, and the climb to riches of Mastro Don Gesualdo, whose name is an ironic comment on his social status–Mastro is a workman who practices an independent trade; Don, a title used in southern Italy to indicate a respected citizen[10]–Verga's *verismo* allows an exceptional insight into the islanders' way of thinking and the cultural implications of Mafioso behavior. Both novels typify Sicilian fatalism, a disposition that paradoxically gives the characters a negative strength apparent in the way they think and respond to tragedy. They also strike, however, a dangerous alliance with a cruel fate that eventually crushes the family's hopes of prosperity.

The important role of the family in Sicilian life and the Mafia gains perspective through the words of police Captain Bellodi, the northern Italian protagonist of Sciascia's *The Day of the Owl,* as he tries to explain the relationship between the family and the law, a relationship central to the understanding of the literature of the island and essential to the thematic development of Giovanni Verga's *I Malavoglia*. Bellodi muses:

> "The family is the Sicilian's state. The state, as it is for us [Northern Italians] is extraneous to them, merely a de facto entity based on force; an entity imposing taxes, military service, war, police. Within the family institution the Sicilian can cross the frontier of his own tragic solitude and fit into a communal life where relationships are governed by hairsplitting contractural ties. To ask him to cross the frontier between family and state would be too much. In imagination he may be carried away by the idea of the State and may even rise to be Prime Minister; but the precise and definite code of his rights and duties will remain within the family, whence the step towards victorious solitude is shorter."[11]

Sciascia's comment is an enlightening assessment of family binding Mafioso style.

I Malavoglia is the first in a projected cycle of five novels Verga called *I Vinti* (*The Vanquished*): *Padron 'Ntoni*, now known as *I Malavoglia*; *Mastro Don Gesualdo*; *La Duchessa delle Gargantas* he later named *La Duchessa di Leyra* a novel that along with *L'Onorevole Scipioni* and *L'uomo di lusso* (*The Wealthy Man*), remains incomplete. As Verga explains, the series was meant to illustrate various stations in life ranging from the pauper, to the legislator, to the artist while exploring "thousands of representations of the human grotesque, providential struggles that guide humanity to the conquest of truth." With this in mind, Verga started the ambitious project that ended after he wrote a few introductory pages to *La Duchessa di Leyra*, the third novel in the series. In a letter to his friend Luigi Capuana, Verga informed him he had trashed the first version of *Padron 'Ntoni* yet he felt at ease with his "bloodless sacrifice" since it gave him greater faith in his work and made him hope that the novel would develop as he had envisioned it in the initial stage. He added: "by the way, have you found a 'ngiuria becoming to my title? What do you think of *I Malavoglia*?"[12] The question of the *'ngiuria* indicated by the family name is important as it gives a clue not only to the novel's subject, but to the meaning *'ngiuria* ("injury") holds in Sicilian jargon and in Mafia parlance. The standard Italian dictionary in Verga's time, *Riguttini-Fanfani*, defines *voglia* as 'an overwhelming desire for something often unattainable.' It also describes it as a *voglia* 'blot' that marks the body of a person. *Voglia*, then, denotes a trait unique to the individual, a blot impossible to erase. *Contro-voglia* or *mala-voglia*, the dictionary specifies also indicates an obligation to do something against one's wishes. In *I Malavoglia* Verga presents a stage full of people marked by a personal *'ngiuria*, nickname often used as an ironic counterpoint on the role the character plays in the narrative. It should be noted that Raymond Rosenthal in his English translation of *I Malavoglia* changes the original title to *The House by the Medlar Tree*, unquestionably one of the novel's most significant symbols as it represents the struggle of Master 'Ntoni and his family to keep the homestead. The English title, however, misses the ironic twist implied by the original where the name of the family is used as *'ngiuria* possibly meaning a scarred destiny, a reference to the fate awaiting them. The Sicilian tradition of using physical and/or personal peculiarities as identification finds an echo in the Mafia where members of the *onorata società* usually go by their nickname.

Verga handles the protagonists of *I Malavoglia* like puppets driven by an unrelenting Darwinian struggle to upgrade their economic condition, an effort that inevitably ends in tragedy. Distant echoes of battles for the unification of Italy during the Risorgimento increase the threat of heavier taxation fueling the skeptical outlook of the islanders toward a future that offers no alternatives to their poverty. In Verga's world characters function in virtue of their attachment to property, the only cause they see as worthy of sacrifice. Ignorance and greed dominate his villagers' ambition hindered by increased taxation on items they need in order to survive, such as salt to preserve the anchovies and pitch to caulk the *paranze*, the fishing boats indispensable to their livelihood. The eldest grandson of Mastro 'Ntoni, young 'Ntoni, returns home from the Navy full of uncertainties and a profound dislike for a life that offers nothing but hardships. Work does not agree with 'Ntoni who gets little solace from the meager wages he receives and sees no justification for his family's dedication to what he considers to be useless sacrifice. His budding relation with Don Franco, the pharmacist, a freethinker and populist, becomes his only solace and makes him scrutinize the oppressive role of authority. Although Don Franco's harangues exceed his courage, he often acts as the story's voice of truth. Don Silvestro, the town clerk, dishonest to the point of cheating the priest's sister Donna Rosolina of her money, fits the description of a rural Mafioso who exercises his power shielded by a corrupt bureaucracy. Don Franco shows to be perceptive when he describes Don Silvestro as: "a real feudal lord, the man of destiny sent on this earth to show how this old society has got to be cleaned up without wasting a minute." Conversely young 'Ntoni Malavoglia, looking for a way out of a life without promise, prompts Don Franco to warn him: "You are the people. As long as you remain as patient as a donkey, you can expect a beating." [13] 'Ntoni's resentment for the miserable circumstances of his life is increased by a desire for riches that takes the form of open rebellion against what he considers the useless sacrifices of his family.

The novel stages a series of events that will become standard elements of defense in several Mafia trials using family honor as a justification for murder. A boat with a cargo of goods is coming from Catania. 'Ntoni and two accomplices plan to rob it in spite of the foul weather and the surveillance of the custom guards commanded by Don Michele. The expedition is a failure. In a futile attempt to escape, 'Ntoni confronted by Don Michele, stabs him in the chest and is arrested by the guards "while all around the bullets were rattling like hailstones." [14] It is here that 'Ntoni, the thief, tied with ropes and prodded along by the soldiers' carbines, becomes a Christ figure. Verga's association of images merely conveys the popular view of the criminal persecuted by the state. Christ, after all, was an outlaw on par with any victim of persecution. 'Ntoni, although culpable, is also a victim of the law imposed by foreign sovereigns–Victor Emmanuel II of Savoy is the last in a long line–thus 'Ntoni's situation is comparable to Christ's, victimized by a foreign power whose representative, Pontius Pilate, had little choice but prosecute him as an enemy of the state. After 'Ntoni's capture, it is the pharmacist who gives perspective to the events: "You want to know who gets caught? The fools get caught." If the culprit, however, has a good lawyer who knows how to take advantage of Sicilian weakness for crimes of passion, he can find a way to demonstrate how the deed–in this case attempted murder–was indispensable to redeem family honor. The whole village knew that Don Michele, commander of the guards, had been courting 'Ntoni's youngest sister Lia, thus 'Ntoni had no choice but avenge this transgression of honorable behavior that cast a shadow on his family.

It is at this point that traditional suspicion of the government and the consequent miscarriage of justice clearly dictate patterns of defense that in the future will become standard for Mafia lawyers eager to exonerate men of honor from legal tangles. Verga assembles a convincing display of *omertà*. Villagers summoned by the court "swear they did not know a thing as true as there is a God! because they did not want to have anything to do with the law." It is Doctor Scipioni, the lawyer hired by Master 'Ntoni to defend his grandson, who presents arguments that in recent years have become a panacea for godfathers suffering from irreparable damage to their honor. Denying the evidence that clearly points to young 'Ntoni as the one who tried to kill Don Michele, Doctor Scipioni, a consummate performer of courtroom melodrama intones:

> "How do you know he [Don Michele] got it [the wound] from 'Ntoni Malavoglia? Can anyone prove it? And who knows whether Don Michele didn't give himself that stab in the belly on purpose, so he could send 'Ntoni Malavoglia to jail?' — Very well, did they want to know the truth? Contraband had absolutely nothing to do with it! There was an old grudge between Don Michele and Master 'Ntoni's 'Ntoni, on account of a woman...They could ask Barbara Zuppidda again, and Comare Venera, and a hundred thousand witnesses, whether it was true or not that Don Michele was having an affair with Lia, 'Ntoni Malavoglia's sister, and hung around Black Lane every evening because of the girl. They'd seen him there the night of the stabbing!"[15]

The lawyer's defense has foreseeable consequences. Young 'Ntoni gets a light sentence, five years in all, while Lia unjustly accused of the worst possible crime in Sicilian rural culture runs away ostracized by the whole village and becomes a prostitute.

Verga in his fictional adaptation of the theme of honor in *I Malavoglia* and in his short story "Cavalleria Rusticana" better known as the libretto of Mascagni's homonymous opera, added considerable alternatives to the repertoire of Mafia strategies. Women and honor became scapegoats for mob murders presumably because the sexual motivation afforded an easy way out. The *onorata società* was living up to its definition making it difficult if not impossible to prosecute murderers obliged by tradition to vindicate the honor of the family trashed by impudent females. Thus in his account of Doctor Scipioni's clever maneuver to get 'Ntoni Malavoglia's sentence reduced, Giovanni Verga while relying on medieval codes of honor established a literary precedent which, along with Compare Alfio's duel to avenge his honor in "Cavalleria Rusticana," would invigorate Mafia strategy. Sciascia explains:

"Ever since the time when, in the sudden silence of the orchestra pit, during Cavalleria Rusticana, the cry of 'Hanno ammazzato compari Turiddu!' ("They've killed Turiddu!') first chilled the spines of opera enthusiasts, criminal statistics and number symbols of the lottery in Sicily have had closer links between cuckoldry and violent death. A crime of passion is solved at once so it is an asset to the police; it is also punished lightly so it is an asset to the mafia." [16]

Thus literature and music cooperate in meeting the needs of the godfathers who found crimes of passions ideal allies in defending their masculine prerogatives and in venting their Mafioso outrage for the insult they had endured.

As for Verga's second novel in the cycle *I Vinti*, *Mastro Don Gesualdo*, the effort of the doomed hero, a mason of humble birth, to accumulate property does not differ much from contemporary Mafia's drive to monopolize profitable *appalti* ("public works"), allocated with the consent of local authorities. The tragedy of Don Gesualdo focuses on his relentless drive to accumulate property, his only purpose in life. As a consequence everything he does becomes poisoned by what seems, and in reality often is, a plot to rob him of his hard earned possessions. Sciascia argues that Verga uses *la roba* as a projection and integration of the individual's personality. Seldom is *la roba* source of income and means of achievement. As wealth grows so does the immediacy of death. "With the growth of wealth what we will leave behind grows as well. The character who accumulates a hoard succumbs under his hoard. The hoard is the reality of death." Blinded by his love for possessions, Don Gesualdo spells his doom. He finds the only moments of peace in the country as he sits outside his farm house in the soft night breeze, waiting for a simple soup of fave, lima beans, and eggs prepared by Diodata (God-given) the faithful servant he has protected and, seemingly, loved more intimately.

At the time Don Gesualdo marries Bianca Trao, the poor descendant of an aristocratic family, he finds a husband for Diodata, Nanni l'Orbo (One-eye John), an unscrupulous servant who gladly takes her with the dowry Don Gesualdo generously, or guiltily, provides. The relationship between the two is somewhat obscured by the numerous subplots woven in the narrative. It emerges again, however, to underscore one of Verga's favorite themes: the use of honor as a weapon to extort property by using veiled allusions easily turned into threats. The night of the insurrection spurred by the Carbonari (members of Giuseppe Mazzini's secret society favoring the annexation of Sicily to the kingdom of Italy)—the Captain of Arms in charge of the troops chooses Don Gesualdo's house as his headquarters. Don Gesualdo is warned by Nardo, an assistant mason, of the possible danger facing him if he returns home as his allegiance to the ruling Bourbons is public knowledge. Don Gesualdo, anticipating party affiliations common to the Mafia, is ultra conservative preferring the status quo encouraged by the Bourbons to a revolutionary regime engaged in land reforms. He feels no one has the right to his property, his only creed or what Sciascia, following D. H. Lawrence's analysis of Verga's self-destructive hero, calls the objective rendition of death.[17] Terrified by the possibility of an arrest, Don Gesualdo seeks shelter in the hut where Nanni l'Orbo and Diodata live and are parents of two sons, Gesualdo named after him and Nunzio.

Diodata, home alone and vulnerable to accusations of adultery, is terrified at the thought that Nanni l'Orbo may come back any moment and find her with her benefactor. If Nanni's reaction to Don Gesualdo's presence in the hut had been uncertain up to now his homecoming dispels all doubts. Aware of having an infallible weapon in his hands, he blurts out: "In all conscience, what you gave me to marry her off is a trifle, in comparison to what you make me look like!" Don Gesualdo, fully aware of Nanni's ploy but unable to counteract capitulates: "What do you want? I'll give you what you want!"...The answer is predictable: "I want my honor, Don Gesualdo! My honor which money can't buy!" Don Gesualdo knows he is trapped. "Do you want the Carmine field?...a piece of land you've been coveting?" Nanni's answer has a typical Mafioso twist "Goddamn. Property helps in emergencies like this...You have put it together, Don Gesualdo, and now it helps you save your hide." [18] Nanni l'Orbo, however, does not live long enough to save his hide and enjoy his profitable transaction.

The next day Mastro Titta is shaving Gerbido, an employee of Baroness Rubiera whose interests constantly clash with Don Gesualdo's, when a man named Canali comes to the door. As Gerbido joins him at the entrance of the house Mastro Titta hears the following exchange: " 'But do you trust him?' And Gerbido answered: 'Oh!!!' 'That's all.'" What is notable about the conversation is the lack of meaning the words convey to any listener unacquainted with the topic. It is a classic example of Mafia's *mezza parola* ("half a word") where the message is characterized by brevity and innuendo accessible only to a party familiar with the subject. Gerbido goes back to finish his shave "and mastro Titta didn't think about it any more." Later on, though, as he sees Gerbido positioned with a gun: "his heart told him that Nanni l'Orbo was the one Gerbido was waiting for." As mastro Titta hears the gun go off the words he had heard before came back to him" and he mutters to himself "I wonder whom that pill is meant for, God save us!"(p. 274) Fully aware of the risk involved if he tells what he knows, Mastro Titta keeps quiet. *Omertà* has the last word and the deadly detonation goes undetected. Nanni l'Orbo's endless demands for *la roba* are stilled forever.

V

The Rise of the Mafia in Sicily's Historical Novel: Pirandello, De Roberto, Lampedusa

Pirandello's (1913–last draft 1931) *I vecchi e i giovani* ("The Old and the Young"); Federico De Roberto's *I Vicerè* (1894) and Tomasi di Lampedusa's *The Leopard* (1958)–the only one of the three novels translated into English–bear witness to Sicily's 1861 annexation to the kingdom of Italy, an event that failed to bring to the island the social reforms and the prosperity Sicilians desperately needed. Luigi Pirandello's *I Vecchi e i Giovani* ("The Old and the Young") is a cynical reminder of the corruption and abuses in post-Risorgimento Italy.[1] In a letter to Ugo Ojetti [2] on December 18, 1908, Pirandello noted:

> "La Rassegna Contemporanea will start publishing a lengthy work of fiction, *I Vecchi e i Giovani*, where I have represented the sad drama of Sicily after 1870. The drama closes with

the events of 1893-94, a terrible year for Italy as it marks the scandalous bankruptcy of the Banca Romana as well as the bankruptcy of traditional patriotism. This is, after all, the year that reveals a true crisis in the growth of our country."

The novel consists of two parts and an *intermezzo*: the first and the second part take place in Sicily, the *intermezzo* in Rome. The Roman *intermezzo* is far from promising for Italy's political future. Actually the corruption in government that culminated in the bankruptcy of the Banca Romana, Rome's most prestigious financial institution, goes a long way to explain the writer's later adherence to Benito Mussolini's Fascist Party that advertised itself as the party of law and order.

The monumental novel published in book form in 1912 deals with events following the Risorgimento, a time when the old generation that had fought under Giuseppe Garibaldi for the annexation of Sicily to Italy no longer felt eager to defend the ideals of its youth. Rather, it was eager to reap financial gains from its political victories. As a consequence, Sicily had relapsed into a state of feudal indolence. Pirandello writes:

> "All social orders in Sicily were dissatisfied with the Italian government in Rome for its complete disinterest in the affairs of the island since 1860...on one side the feudal tradition persisted, the habit of treating the *contadini* [laborers in the field] like beasts using avarice and usury to keep them in line; on the other side, the inveterate, ferocious hatred of land owners and an absolute lack of trust in justice."

This atmosphere of greed and social injustice animates the drama of the Fasci Siciliani dei Lavoratori, a socialist organization meant to protect the rights of the workers, in this case the sulfur miners, near Girgenti (Agrigento), victims of greedy owners who turned them into human robots under working conditions unfit for slave labor. The young who wanted social reforms believed that finally in a unified Italy Sicilian youth till then vainly sacrificed "could shake the outrageous oppression of the old...and claim itself victorious." [3]

In the novel, the Mafia is mentioned in relation to the upcoming elections for Parliamentary representatives in Rome. Exponents of the *alta Mafia* linked to the Mason agitators subdivided into "Lodges" with a supreme commander known as the "Great Teacher" were sent to Girgenti to pave the way for a popular election aimed to diminish, or more accurately, to demolish the power of the aristocracy and the church. Pirandello's criticism does not spare the aristocracy, greedy and secure in its own birthrights, nor the Catholic Church, concerned with its vast properties and special privileges. Actually it is hard to find a character or political view spared from authorial criticism. Typically, the strategy of the Mafia is to side with the party or individual best qualified to serve its interests in the government. The idealism that had inspired so many Sicilians to fight for the annexation of the island to the kingdom of Italy during the Risorgimento is rejected in favor of self-serving ambition and the increase of personal property. The realization of the betrayal inflicted on men of integrity who sacrificed their lives for an ideal increasingly soiled by greed and lust for power finds its avatar in Mauro Mortara, a simple, honest man who fought in Milazzo with general Garibaldi and is now guardian of the feud of Valsania near Girgenti (Agrigento). Mauro keeps a small museum of memorabilia celebrating Sicily's successful fight against the kingdom of the Due Sicilie, so named as Sicily and Naples were under Bourbon rule till Sicily cut its ties following the arrival of Garibaldi and his "Thousand" in 1860. At last, Mauro gets the chance to fulfill his life-long dream and go to Rome to see "the eternal city," cradle of Italy's glorious past. Betrayed in his most cherished ideals when confronted with the corruption in the government he helped create, Mauro Mortara goes back to Valsania, dons his uniform of *garibaldino* and in an ironic twist of fate is killed by the very soldiers sent from Rome to stifle the insurrection of the *solfarai* in the sulphur mines near Girgenti. Astonished by the decorations they see on the chest of the dying man, the soldiers' exchange glances and in their mind formulate the question that ends the novel "Chi avevano ucciso?" ("Who had they killed?") The question remains unanswered giving readers the opportunity to fill in their own conclusion. And the conclusion can only be that Mauro Mortara and his idealistic patriotism are the victims of dishonesty, plotting, the ineptitude of the central government and of a local administration infiltrated by profiteers with close ties to the *alta Mafia*.

As Sciascia claims in *Pirandello e la Sicilia*, [4] the novel is especially poignant as it was born from Pirandello's personal experience. The sulphur mines near Girgenti, property of his father and the family of his wife, were flooded in 1897 and rendered totally useless. The disaster ruined both families and forced Luigi and his bride, Antonietta Portulano, to move to Rome where he found a position teaching composition at the Istituto Superiore di Magistero, a teacher institute. Antonietta became increasingly despondent and eventually had to be placed under constant surveillance in a facility for the mentally ill.

Madness, faked or real, emerged as one of the main themes in Pirandello's fiction. His analysis of the absurdities of the human condition exemplified by characters victimized by social conventions became the unmistakable signature of the writer who, near death, requested that his ashes be taken to his birth place near Agrigento lu Causu ("Chaos") where they rest inside a Greek jar placed on top of a console in the family house. Pirandello's choice of burial site was appropriate. Punning on his reputation for making fake or real madness the subject of so many plays and novels, he referred to himself as "the son of Chaos."

Pirandello's vast array of novels, plays and short stories deal with individuals whose freedom is threatened by conventions or legal constrictions that must be defied in order to avoid infringement on individual rights. In many instances the Pirandellian individual has no choice but break with the law to find fulfillment. Thus Liolà, the main character who names the play, fathers children but avoids marriage to keep free from legal entanglements. In "The Jar," one of Pirandello's best known short stories, the legalistic mind of wealthy Don Lollò clashes with the peasant stubbornness of Zi' Dima as he forces him to mend from the inside a giant crater for olive oil that accidentally had split in two, instead of letting him apply a cement of his own making from the outside. Don Lollò's stubbornness proves disastrous. Zi' Dima remains sealed inside the treacherous belly of the jar—a rigid, inflexible form resistant to the flow of life. A staunch believer in the rights of the law, Don Lollò seeks advice from his lawyer who welcomes the tale of the strange mishap with an uncontrollable burst of laughter. There are no alternatives. If Zi' Dima is to be freed, the form must be broken. Thus the inevitable happens. Don Lollò victim of his own rage shoves the jar down the slope and watches it smash against an olive tree as Zi' Dima, appropriately described as an ancient Saracen olive log, emerges triumphant from the broken crater.

What makes Pirandello's narrative so very Sicilian in nature is his representation of the law as an enemy of the individual, an incarcerating force that must be defeated in order to survive. Legalism can entrap the individual and destroy the right to personal independence. Freedom, then, consists in the ability to repudiate the binds of conventional behavior dictated by society. Needless to say, this is the starting point of the Mafioso cry for non-interference from legal authorities. Often the price for this individual choice is solitude. Such is the case of Mattia Pascal in the novel, *Il Fu Mattia Pascal*. The would-be-drowned Mattia Pascal, who has assumed the false identity of Adriano Meis, must die again to resume his former identity and his place in society. At his return home he finds himself an outcast deprived of family ties because his wife has remarried. He is denied reinstatement in a community that finds his return from the dead inconvenient, thus he is relegated to a life of oblivion in the company of an aunt. Understandably puzzled by his strange destiny, he is enlightened by an old priest, Don Eligio, who points out that no one can be somebody outside the law. Thus Mattia Pascal has no alternative but accept his peculiar status of non-existence.

Even more poignant is the drama of *Henry IV* protagonist of the drama, who chooses isolation and the stigma of madness over a society steeped in conventions and hypocrisy. He becomes an outlaw protected from legal interferences by his fiction, but is doomed to a life of solitude, a prisoner of the mask he himself has created. Pirandello's anti-legalistic view is not so different from that of many Sicilians who traditionally have looked on the trappings of the law either with hatred, as is the case with the Mafioso, or with fear and distrust, as is the case with many islanders unjustly persecuted. Considering the island's history and its struggle with legislation imposed by conquerors or conveniently adapted to suit the needs of foreign authorities and local Mafia bosses, Pirandello's anarchic view, far from being rationalized to reach extreme conclusions, is reasonable, at least by Sicilian standards.

As for *I Vecchi e i Giovani* ("The Old and the Young"), the novel strikes a personal note because the inspiration is largely autobiographical. Antonio del Re, the idealist who goes to Rome to promote the Socialist cause, has been seen as an alter ego for Pirandello. Other characters in the novel seem to have been patterned after members of the writer's family. Pirandello chooses the strike of the *solfarai* in the sulphur mines near Agrigento along with the formation of the Fasci Siciliani dei Lavoratori, to convey the painful rite of passage from Bourbon rule to the House of Savoy along with the disillusionment experienced by most Sicilians during the twenty three years (1870-93) that followed. In *Pirandello e la Sicilia*, Sciascia points out that *The Old and the Young* is the only work where Pirandello mentions the Mafia as a behind the scenes operational force that along with the Masons manipulates local elections. It seems worthwhile to examine the context where the reference appears. The passage relates a conversation between Prince Ippolito Laurentano and Don Illuminato Lagaipa (here Don means Reverend), an old friend of the Prince who comes to announce the visit of an influential churchman, Monsignor Montoro, eager to discuss the coming elections where Girgenti's (Agrigento) representative in Rome will be selected. During an emotional speech filled with apocalyptic premonitions, Don Lagaipa warns Prince Laurentano:

> "Looks like the horns of the accursed devil are itching... War...war...tempest! I hear that following the request of the canonico Agrò [a priest who supervises doctrinal questions]...two famous ambassadors at the command of the alta mafia [the mafia's ruling body] and of a well known mason group have arrived from Palermo..."

The prince, enraged by the news, proposes to fight to the end this threat to his privileged caste. Obliging but skeptical, Don Lagaipa resumes: "the Mafia is now involved...the police favors all kinds of evil maneuvers. There is more to add. An important man...a deputato, Selmi, I think..." The prince interrupts the priest's incoherent recital and in a mood of nostalgia evokes the memory of Filangieri, an envoy of the Bourbon rulers, who had been successful in repressing the Sicilian uprising of 1848 and had proceeded to restore what the prince sees as the proper social order after sixteen months of "obscene revolutionary orgy." He further recalls that "the feeling of revulsion he had experienced in those sixteen months had remained vivid in [his]...recollections mostly because of the brutal menace of the populace to the privileges of the aristocracy and to the religious tradition"[5] The situation Pirandello describes here points to the alliance between the feudal aristocracy and the Catholic Church. The allusion is quite revealing. It clearly illustrates the conservative position of the clergy and the aristocracy while the Mafia lurks in the background, an opportunistic ally of the side most likely to win, or even better, of the side that can promote its financial and political goals. Pirandello shows quite clearly that profit and power remain the lasting aim of political success. This is the reason why Mauro Mortara dies in vain. Idealism and politics don't mix.

Pirandello's *I Vecchi e i Giovani* deals with the irony of human history doomed to repeat itself and find its most fragile targets in the weak, the poor and the idealistic. The young are not much different from the old. It is their youth that makes them passionate, daring and eager to forge ahead. Eventually the mistakes of the old are duplicated and personal interests obliterate a genuine passion for reform. Pirandello unfolds a vast panorama of Sicily's frenzied history as he readies to direct his drama among the ruins of Girgenti's Greek temples and Rome's deceitful past glory. The cast is as huge as the mise en scene: the aristocracy faithful to the Bourbons and to their inherited rights is championed by Prince Ippolito di Laurentano who views the 1848 revolution as a disruption of the proper social order. The Catholic Church goes hand in hand with the aristocracy in an effort to curb the cycle of history that is about to turn in a direction contrary to its interests. The Mafia, unhindered by scruples or idealistic motives, has seized the advantage of changing times. Lack of commitment to moral principles enables the *onorata società* to become involved in the political process catering to popular causes as a sure way to gain political clout. Incidences of violence, false promises, and political abuses following the annexation of Sicily to the kingdom of Italy stand witness to the failure of the Risorgimento in the island. The naive assumption of the Piedmontese administration that Sicilians could effect a smooth transition from a deeply rooted skepticism in human justice to a new regime that promises a fair share in the future of the nation showing little understanding of local problems, proves to be a miscalculation at best. The Piedmonteses are too far removed by geography and tradition from the Sicilians to see through the masquerade of political elections regularly rigged by powerful *galantuomini* ("honest men"). The fact remains that things were not going to change as the political influence of the Mafia was growing beyond all expectations—even beyond the wildest expectations of its most prominent members.

Another epic saga dealing with the twenty seven years that saw the transition from Bourbon rule to new political trends, 1855 to 1882, is Federico De Roberto's *I VICERÈ* (1894) where the struggle of a powerful aristocratic family of Spanish descent, the Uzeda former Viceroys of Sicily, to secure the largest share of the inheritance left by the family matriarch, Donna Teresa Uzeda Risá, Princess of Francalanza[6] reveals a ruthless struggle for wealth and political leverage. As the novel begins Teresa Uzeda has succumbed to a fatal illness and is now the object of an elaborate ritual, as was customary in Sicily to commemorate the death of a member of a powerful family. The celebrations to honor Donna Uzeda include flowery epitaphs, a high mass composed by local musicians, a huge crowd of relatives hoping to profit from the princess' will, aristocrats convened from the three corners of Sicily, *lavapiatti* ("dish washers")–a moniker for impoverished relatives looking for a hand out–and an eager populace attracted to the spectacle by the same fascination it experienced watching the Inquisition's *auto da fe* abolished by Domenico Caracciolo, Viceroy of Sicily (1782), without regard for the populace robbed of its favorite entertainment.

The princess had died a natural death comforted by the sacraments of mother church eagerly administered by the monks of the convent of the Capuchins who had vastly profited from her generosity. Following her wish to be mummified, the monks placed her remains in the vault of their necropolis as an inspiration to all and a lasting symbol of family power. Death in the Uzeda family turns into a public spectacle celebrating the importance of wealth fiercely contested by the living whose only aim is to preserve and multiply their share of property. Partition of the inheritance sparks a family war and bares long seething hatreds waiting to be unveiled at the least provocation. De Roberto chooses the disclosure of the will to characterize the children and their relationship to their defunct mother. As they sit in the palace's Gallery of Portraits waiting to hear the testament of the *felice memoria* ("happy memory") as the Princess is referred to, a huge portrait of Sicily's Viceroy, Lopez Ximenes Uzeda, hangs behind the eldest son's shoulders, riding a horse in the act of stopping the animal with his left hand as if to warn "I am the boss here!" The portrait's prediction proves correct even if the prince is not alone in becoming the boss since his mother, in a quirky decision prompted by favoritism, left the bulk of the inheritance for him to share with her favorite youngest son, Count Raimondo, whom she had purposely married to a minor member of the Sicilian aristocracy to afford him the freedom to enjoy women and gambling in Florence without his wife having the possibility to protest his libertine behavior.

The rest of the princess' children, a sizeable group of ecclesiastics, half-wits and daughters, all filled with expectations that in most cases go unfulfilled, anxiously wait for Signor Marco, the executor of the will, to announce their share in the family fortune. Disappointment is inevitable. Since Giacomo XIV, Prince of Francalanza, and Count Raimondo are named universal heirs, the rest of the family is left only the crumbs from the feast. According to the "happy memory," the children professed to religious life have been assured a reward much greater than any earthly benefit. Yet, even here, favoritism plays a part. Lodovico, aka Father Benedict of the Convent of San Nicola in Catania, receives the mere pittance of thirty-six *onze*, while Angiolina, aka Sister Maria Crocifissa, is assigned two thousand *onze* for her filial obedience, as she had taken religious vows to please her mother. The last son, Ferdinando, who followed the stoic example of Robinson Crusoe and farmed a plot of land rented from his mother, was left "The Acorns" as his property without the obligation of paying the arrears. Chiara and Lucrezia, the two remaining daughters, received ten thousand *onze* each. In addition Chiara was left the family jewels as a token of her mother's benevolence.

The partition of property is not seen well by everyone especially by Don Blasco, brother of the defunct husband of the princess, a corrupt Benedictine monk residing in the convent of San Nicola where, as well known in Sicilian history, financial and sexual abuses had been going on for centuries. The complex web of names and characters bringing the cast of *I Vicerè* to life include Donna Ferdinanda, a confirmed old maid, whose fanaticism for the aristocratic tradition of the Uzeda and lust for property become a paradox as she amasses a fortune by charging high interest rates for small loans to indigent people feeling that her birthright justifies her extortionist tactics.

The family's struggle for the inheritance evolves side by side with tumultuous historical events. General Garibaldi's defeat of Francis II in Naples gives Sicily fresh hope nourished by patriotic fervor, some of it genuine. Freedom, however, has always eluded Sicily, a land too often deceived by what appeared to be a promising alternative. De Roberto shares his pessimism with the reader through a scathing analysis of the events and a penetrating psychological study of the characters. As the day of the elections approaches and the hope of annexation to Italy's new kingdom is at its highest, Chiara Uzeda is about to give birth to the heir she and her husband have desired with a passion. The scene is shown through a lens that allows double exposure each portraying an image of aborted hope and falsified expectations. Chiara groans as her body contracts to expel the fetus from the womb. As the baby finally comes into sight, one of the midwives cries out in horror: "What is it?" The answer comes sudden and terrifying as the creature is fully expelled: "From the bleeding cavity a piece of formless flesh was coming out, a thing that could not be described, a fish with a beak, a bird devoid of feathers. The sexless monster had only one eye, three different paws and was still alive." This aberration of nature caught in an evolutionary stage, is subliminally related to the ancient symbol of Sicily, the Trinacria: three naked legs racing around the head of the snake-infested head of a Gorgon placed at the center of the group.[7] The fetus dies immediately. The women assisting Chiara try to hide the monster wrapping it up in a blanket. Chiara, however, insists on seeing it. As she glances at the listless body she is not shocked nor does she cry. She calmly orders her maid to bring a large jar filled with alcohol meant to become the repository of the creature placed inside the container by the consenting father. A sarcastic comment ends the incident: "the others left one by one leaving Chiara alone with her husband staring with satisfaction at the anatomical display, the latest product of the race of the Vicerè"

De Roberto carries the incident further, devising a political *contrapasso* ("counterpart") outside the palace of the Uzedas where another monstrous birth is in progress during a popular demonstration to elect the Duke of Oragua as first Representative to the Italian Parliament. The Duke, "yellow as a corpse," incapable of addressing the populace screaming beneath the balcony, finally utters a few words as the crowd, intoxicated by its own enthusiasm, is leaving. The Prince of Francalanza, who has been watching the Duke's inept public performance, has a telling conversation with his son Consalvo, a small boy at the time. "See how they [the people] respect your uncle? How the whole town favors him?" The boy, a little stunned by the noise, asked: "What does Deputato mean?" He replies, "Deputati are those who make laws in the Parliament" His son then asks, "Does the king make laws?" The Prince of Francalanza then says, "The king and the Representatives together. After all, the king can't do everything. You can see how your uncle [the Duke of Oragua] brings honor to his family. When the Vicerè were in power, members of our family were Vicerè, now that we have a Parliament, your uncle is Representative!" [8] Aborted freedom is preserved with the same care Chiara uses in preserving the monstrous fetus. The status quo will dominate the Sicilian political scene giving the ruling class the advantages it always enjoyed and the Mafia the control of the island's developing industries.

The young scion of the Uzedas, Prince Consalvo, quickly learns the art of political manipulation. Perceptive, self-centered and power hungry he becomes convinced that the only guideline worth following is his personal gain. Being a member of the powerful Uzeda family, he is endowed with special privileges that government and religious authorities can not take away. Thus Consalvo is destined to be the new man, the new leader, and idol of the people. As leader his greatest asset is not his exalted position nor his money, but his ability to use rhetoric to his advantage in the great Sicilian oratorical tradition, redundant perhaps, nevertheless effective. Thus when the time comes for Parliamentary elections, Consalvo, Prince of Francalanza, is ready. A true Machiavellian, he knows only too well that social and political inequalities will always exist: "someone clever will always, any time, under any type of government cheat the simple and the bold, stop the timid and the strong, overcome the weak." To frustrate the attacks of his opponents who call him Signor Principe, Mr. Prince, he insists to be called Consalvo Uzeda.[9]

When Consalvo feels threatened by political opposition he turns to the companions of his riotous youth, the local *bassa Mafia*, a medley of thugs ready to fight at the slightest provocation. At this juncture, De Roberto offers a clue of what will become a requirement for aspiring Mafiosi. As already noted, they must commit at least one murder to become members of the organization while godfathers, protected by their powerful position, manage political and financial operations from a safe distance immune to the consequences. Although in the novel the alliance between the prince and the Mafia is merely a convenient arrangement, the connection between the Mafia and powerful political interests is already present.

The day of the electoral caucus, candidate Consalvo Uzeda makes his debut among the frantic cheers of the public easily charmed by his eloquence. The approval is partly due to the prince's willingness to speak in public, thus eliminating any discrimination against plain citizens. The sight chosen for the meeting is the Benedictine monastery where Consalvo went to school. Although recently laicized, the monastery remains a symbol of his former social status. Among cries of "Long live Francalanza" ("Long live democracy"), Consalvo goes into a long-winded historical survey spiced by invocations to Italy's glorious past. The oratorical bravura of the would-be Deputato goes on beyond the endurance of even the most enthusiastic followers. He finally winds up the performance to shouts of "Hail Francalanza! Hail our Deputato!" and assurances that he will become Sicily's first Representative elected by the people. Buoyed by his success Consalvo starts calling on his aristocratic relatives. Last in his list is aunt Ferdinanda, the old maid, confined to bed with a cavernous cough. Although fully aware that his concern for her health is prompted by the hope to become her heir she agrees to see him. It is at this point that Consalvo, still elated by his recent success, loses all restrains and discloses his true feelings in the speech that closes the novel.

Following a preamble where he admits that the past is always preferable to the present mostly because the past is no longer here, he recalls his uncle, the Duke of Oragua, and his pragmatic acceptance of a new reality when he was named first Sicilian representative to the Italian Parliament. The memory leads Consalvo to explain his political views based on the belief that, in politics, immobility is better than change since history is a monotonous repetition of the past. Men have been, are, and always will be the same. Conditions, however, change. There seems to be an abyss between feudal Sicily as it was before 1860 and the present. The difference, however, can be seen only on the surface. Consalvo shares this perception with Machiavelli who in *The Prince* warns: "I believe that the man who adapts his course of action to the nature of the times will succeed and, likewise, that the man who sets his course of action out of tune with the times will come to grief," [10] a view he reiterates in *The Discourses* where he insists:

"Since human affairs are constantly changing and never remain fixed, it is necessary that they either rise or fall, and many things that you are not impelled to do by reason you are impelled to do by necessity."[11]

The ability to recognize determining factors in a move politically motivated is the main ingredient in retaining power. Actually Consalvo Uzeda detests change, the status quo is more convenient and more profitable. Sicily's new politicians are not new to the game. They are the same powerful, wealthy men recycled to fit an image that suits their purpose. The only innovation is the slogans, modernized, democratized, and polished with new clichés. What is important for the Prince and the landowners in general is to retain their wealth and their position of leadership in the new government. Like the fetus of Chiara Uzeda, the birth of the new Sicily is a symbol of corrupted fertility preserved for generations to come.

The family of the Vicerè in its reactionary drive for power fits only too well Francesco Renda's evaluation of the conservative nature of the Mafia. The senator from Agrigento writes:

"Mafioso feeling is not inclined to modify the organization of society. It leans instead toward keeping intact positions already achieved: it is therefore a passive form of resistance that endows it with greater vitality."[12]

As we have seen Judge Rocco Chinnici shortly before being murdered updated the situation by describing the Mafia as "a tragic, relentless, cruel vocation to get rich." A vocation, incidentally that fits Corrado Uzeda, scion of Spanish Vicerè as well as Mastro Don Gesualdo Motta, Verga's hard working mason who makes his debut in local society holding his brand new hat "with his lime eaten hands."[13]

Writing in the same historical time frame Giuseppe di Lampedusa introduces another prince, Tancredi Falconeri, penniless but endowed with charisma, intelligence, ambition and the admiration and protection of his powerful uncle, the Prince of Salina. He too will overcome all obstacles and gain wealth and political clout by basing his strategy on cynical pragmatism symbolized by his well-known remark: "if we want things to stay as they are, things will have to change." Long before the Prince of Falconeri took shape in the imagination of Giuseppe di Lampedusa, De Roberto's prince Consalvo Uzeda had discovered the advantages of adapting to changing times and of seizing new political opportunities. The name of the game was changing but the game, in Mafia parlance, remained *la stessa cosa* played by clever, unscrupulous individuals eager to manipulate and compromise the welfare of the Sicilian people in order to increase access to the central government in Rome and tighten their hold on property.

The surrealistic quality of Sicilian tradition becomes a paradoxical *memento mori* (loosely translated as "remember you are going to die") in the catacombs of Palermo's church of the Capuchins where eight-thousand mummified cadavers of the clergy and wealthy Palermitans hang on walls or rest in boxes in a grim rendez-vous of a *cosca* pledged to eternal silence. A small cemetery outside the church houses, the remains of distinguished Palermitans forced into a far less sensational display of their remains by legislation issued in 1881 forbidding mummification of corpses. The cemetery attendant explained to this writer that a well-known Sicilian author and his wife were buried there. As a steady drizzle made the dust on the tombstones roll in small opaque balls down the marble slabs, he stopped in front of a marker void of decorations. Two names were sculpted on the surface: Giuseppe Tomasi Principe di Lampedusa and his wife's, Alessandra Wolff Stomersee, Principessa di Lampedusa. Even if kept at some distance from the mummified skeletons hanging in the crypt, Giuseppe and Alessandra di Lampedusa were faithful enough to the tradition of Palermo's aristocracy to be buried in the cemetery of the Capuchins. In a moment of ironic assessment of his approaching death Prince Fabrizio Salina, Lampedusa's alter ego in *The Leopard*, expresses his regret for the passing tradition:

> "A pity corpses could not be hung up by the neck in the crypt and watched slowly mummifying; he would look magnificent on that wall, tall and big as he was, terrifying girls by the set smile on his sandpaper face, by his long, long white pique trousers. But no, they would dress him up in party clothes, perhaps in this very evening coat he was wearing now"[14]

His sarcasm was on target. Fabrizio of Salina clearly knew that the wheels of history were turning away from his caste replacing the avid aristocracy that for centuries had ruled Sicily with the murderous greed of the Mafia. His keen sense of history and his respect for family tradition made his choice of burial place a testament to a world that was fast disappearing.

As should become increasingly clear, political stability has never been one of Sicily's strongest characteristics. The island's tumultuous history is ample testimonial to the reluctance of politicians and ruling classes to change their ways. The prestige conferred by wealth and power is an advantage never undervalued by the Mafia. As a result the leit-motif of *The Leopard*, spoken by Tancredi Falconeri, the Prince's favorite nephew: "If we want things to stay as they are, things will have to change"[15] rings with a clever truthfulness that deserves the approval of Machiavelli. The theme of *The Leopard* in many ways is similar to that of the other fiction already examined. Here, however, *la roba* is used to highlight a change of the guard as Mafioso feeling is shrewdly employed to instill a patriotic fervor suitable to the historical circumstances.

Lampedusa's use of literary sources is subtle and effective: Ariostotle, Tasso, Machiavelli, Montaigne, and Baudelaire are fused with superb stylistic skill in illustrating and bringing to a close an era when the Sicilian aristocracy was responsible for its behavior to God alone. The novel focuses on important social and political changes that take place during the critical days of Garibaldi's invasion. The action of the novel spans from 1860-61 with an aftermath in 1910, long after Prince Fabrizio Salina is deceased and his spinster daughters, Concetta, Carolina and Caterina worship false religious relics, pathetic reminders of an age that is itself a relic. Allusions to allied bombardments in Sicily during WW II update the historical framework of the novel inserting in the narrative a reminder of humanity's drive to self-destruct.

At the start of the novel Prince Fabrizio Salina is profiled in the fullness of his manhood. It is the time of the Spedizione dei Mille. After landing near Marsala Giuseppe Garibaldi and his volunteers proceeded to occupy the island in the name of Victor Emmanuel II, king of Piedmont and Sardinia and by now King of Italy. The King proposed new rules to make the annexation of Sicily a reality through representation of *deputati* elected by the people. The Piedmontese chose to be persuasive rather than violent. Sicilians, after all, had fought side by side with the soldiers of Garibaldi in a well-meant effort to make Sicily an integral part of the mainland. Prince Fabrizio Salina is too skeptical and world wise to accept the invitation to take an active part in the new government. His historical vision is conditioned by a long tradition that obscures Sicily's future with a curtain of past experiences impervious to innovations. "Till there is death there is hope" muses the Prince,[16] a tranquilizing slogan since it allows him to observe the situation from an Olympian distance. The wheels of history keep turning without affecting his enlightened pessimism or his awareness that the ongoing rite of passage is filled with ominous implications for his class and its descendants. Prince Fabrizio Salina's perspective, gained through his fatalistic view of life, erases uncertainties that can interfere with what ironically could be called his past vision of the future. It is the vision of someone who meets the ultimate truth refusing to give up life's most exquisite gratifications.

It seems useful to compare the Kafkaesque end of Lampedusa's *The Leopard* to Pirandello's *The Old and the Young*, mostly to point out the symbolic intimation of hopelessness that links the two novels. It may be recalled that Mauro Mortara, Pirandello's aging *garibaldino*, returns from Rome a broken man after having witnessed the corruption of the new Italy he has helped create. The remembrance of the days when he fought for the annexation of Sicily to the mainland drives him to shed tears of despair as he seeks refuge in the old *camerone*, a large chamber filled with mementos of his adventurous life. In a corner, hardly visible, he discerns "the melancholy stuffed leopard without one eye" he had begged in Africa when he was young "[he] had not been able to show [to the leopard] how many cobwebs held him against the wall, how much dust had collected on its fur now spotted with globs of mildew."[17] What at one time had been a splendid animal was now reduced to a pelt deteriorating as quickly as Mauro's hopes for the future of Sicily. Giuseppe di Lampedusa's *The Leopard* closes with a similar incident symbolized in this case by the dusty carcass of Bendicò, the beloved Great Dane of the deceased Prince of Salina, embalmed for forty five years and finally cast from a window by order of his daughter, Princess Concetta, who symbolically renounces the last relic of a past forever gone. As the fur floats in midair on its way to the garbage heap, the novel reaches its climactic end:

> "During the flight his form [Bendicò's] re-composed himself for an instant; in the air one could have seen dancing a quadruped with long whiskers, and its right foreleg seemed to be raised in imprecation. Then all found peace in a heap of livid dust."[18]

The heraldic symbol of the House of Salina, a leopard, is by now ancient history. What remains is a different order that has lived and prospered in the background, its intentions fully understood by discerning men like the Prince who, however, was pragmatic enough to accommodate the nouveau riches increasingly in charge of the land and the future of Sicily. The leopards were dying. It was a natural death due to a stalemate in the evolutionary process. Only fools like Pirandello's Mauro Mortara could be idealistic enough to die for a cause that no longer existed. The smart ones had learned their lesson: Tancredi, the Prince of Salina's pragmatic nephew and local members of the *onorata società* knew only too well–as Tancredi liked to say–"if we want things to stay as they are, things will have to change." Tancredi clearly was aware that if the aristocracy was to survive, an alliance with the wealthy newcomers was inevitable.

The Leopard opens with an invocation to Mary, mother of God, to assist sinners "*nunc et in hora mortis nostrae*" ("now and at the hour of our death") as the Prince's family gathers to recite the rosary performed with appropriate composure by the Prince, assisted in his religious duties by Father Pirrone, the Jesuit chaplain assigned to the household by the Bishop to honor the important place the Salinas held in the Sicilian aristocracy. The opening sentence establishes the novel's thematic continuity. "Death is not an evil but a certitude ready to strike without notice." This truism is first detected in nature as the Prince philosophizes in the garden over the pungent bouquet of smells that blends intoxicating odors with the nauseous scent of decay generated by the body of a young *garibaldino* soldier by now removed, who a month earlier had dragged himself to die in the voluptuous garden of the Salinas where overripe fruits and huge scarlet roses evoked sensual excesses.

Concerned with the safety of the women living in the palace in the event of a forced entry by Garibaldi's revolutionary troops, Fabrizio di Salina approaches his accountant, Don Ciccio Ferrara, administrator of the Prince's vast fortune. The Prince is perfectly aware that Don Ciccio besides his wages enjoys other incomes by skimming the revenues from his lands. Increasingly irritated for being treated like a fool, the Prince looks over "the huge registers" carefully kept by Don Ciccio: "in them, with two years' delay, were inscribed in minute writing all the Salina accounts, except for the really important ones." [19] The exception makes the rule. The administrator is stealing, taking advantage of the passive nature of the Prince who finds the notion of arguing about money not only demeaning but out of his range of interests. Mulling over Don Ciccio's intentions as he would surely represent the class which would now be gaining power, the Prince goes on to speculate that "the glorious new days for this Sicily of ours"–as proclaimed by the administrator–"have been promised us on every single one of the thousand invasions we've had from Nicias onward, and they've never come. And why should they come, anyway? Oh, well. Just negotiations punctuated by a little harmless shooting, then all will be the same though all will be changed." [20] The scene is repeated during the Prince's conversation with Russo "the most significant of his dependents...a perfect specimen of a class on its way up." With the confidence of an insider, Russo assures the Prince that his nephew Tancredi, fighting at present with the Piedmontese, will be back sooner than expected. He allows that "there will be a day or two of shooting and trouble, but Villa Salina will be safe as a rock; Your Excellency is our Father, I have many friends here. The Piedmontese will come cap in hand to pay Your Excellencies their respects." [21] The Prince is too wise to refuse the help of Russo although he feels humiliated to be protected by the many friends of a dependent who robs him blind while proclaiming his allegiance. The real shocker, however, comes when the whole family goes to spend a few months in the feud of Donnafugata where the Prince learns of the enormous wealth of Don Calogero Sedara, a self-made man obviously expert in making profitable deals. Don Calogero had taken over the property of Baron Tumino who had faulted the mortgage on his estate, he had also purchased some land rich in a very profitable type of stone, and he had taken advantage of the famine following the landing of Garibaldi to make an excellent profit on the sale of wheat. In short, he was rich. Don Onofrio Rotolo, the steward of Donnafugata, honest to a fault, explains to the Prince: "I've totted it up roughly on my fingers: Don Calogero's income will very shortly be equal to that of Your Excellency here at Donnafugata." He further informs the Prince:

> "Don Calogero is now the leader of the liberals in town and other districts nearby with every chance to be elected to the Parliament in Turin in the next elections. His daughter, Angelica, just got back from school in Florence and goes around town in a crinoline and with velvet ribbons hanging from her hat"[22]

Angelica eventually makes a breathtaking appearance at Donnafugata ensnaring with her charms the Prince who, like

Charlemagne and the knights in Ariosto's Orlando Furioso, is captivated by her beauty. [23] Tancredi, who is on a brief leave from military duties, finds Angelica and her huge dowry irresistible. He wins her hand without difficulty, trading his title of Prince of Falconeri for Angelica's father, Don Calogero Sedara, remarkable fortune. As events favor his most ambitious plans, Don Calogero's main concern is to keep the rest of his family at large. His wife, Donna Bastiana, a peasant woman of great beauty and fathomless ignorance, is, according to Don Ciccio the Prince's hunting companion, "a kind of animal" kept out of the public eye to facilitate the ambitious plans of Don Calogero for the future of Angelica. Don Ciccio's revelations become even more appalling:

> "Don Calogero's wife is the daughter of one of your peasants from Runci, Peppe Giunta...so filthy and so savage that everyone called him Peppe 'Mmerda, [Peppe Shit] excuse the word, Excellency. Don Calogero, a master at doing away with obstacles, felt perfectly justified in eliminating Peppe 'Mmerda. Angelica's grandfather was found dead near Rampinzeri with twelve bullets in the kidney"[24]

Once his father-in-law disappeared Don Calogero's ascent knew no boundaries as his wealth made his manners irrelevant. Under the tutelage of his future son-in-law Tancredi, whose humorous surveillance spares him unforgivable gaffes, he makes exceptional progress. Actually the Prince, who possesses an unusual amount of equanimity, develops a great deal of admiration for Don Calogero Sedara's business sense. He is the new man who will achieve power because of his ruthlessness and irreversible greed. As Mayor of Donnafugata, Don Calogero–who has been granted the title of Barone del Biscotto (Baron of the Biscuit) by His Majesty Ferdinand IV for some work he had done in the port of Mazzara–is in charge of the Plebiscite [25] constituted to make the annexation of Sicily to the kingdom of Italy official. There are the usual foreign faces from Girgenti in the tavern of Zzu Menico "where they were declaiming about the 'magnificent and progressive future of the new Sicily' united to resurgent Italy."[26] In the referendum the Prince votes yes for the annexation not out of conviction but because he thinks, quite correctly, that there are no alternatives. The Bourbon rulers are finished and the kingdom of Italy is a reality that cannot be denied.

The result of the election at Donnafugata stands as an affirmation of the people's unanimous acceptance of the new regime: "voters listed, 515; voted, 512; yes, 512; no zero" [27] except that Don Ciccio, the Prince's hunting companion, had good memories of the generosity of the Bourbon king towards his family and voted no. The dissenting vote was eliminated. Sedara is ruthless, greedy, impossible to defeat—shortly the prototype of the powerful godfather ready to take over where the weak aristocracy has failed. His feeling, understated but always present, is the best guarantee of his dedication to Sicily's unification with Italy. The Prince has no illusions. He knows very well that his beloved nephew Tancredi is too smart to be left behind. By his marriage to the wealthy Angelica Sedara his future is assured.

The moment of truth comes when a representative of the Piedmontese government, Aimone Chevalley di Monterzuolo, is sent from Turin to see the Prince hoping to persuade him to become a senator in the government of Victor Emmanuel II. Torn between the fear of "the bearded faces of the armed keepers standing about in the first courtyard" and admiration for the splendid decor of the Prince's residence, Chevalley of Monterzuolo receives a gracious welcome that dispels his uneasy first impression. The Piedmontese envoy finds in the Prince an unexpected reticence and a sincere desire for clarifications. Declaring complete ignorance of the duties performed by a senator, the Prince elicits an enthusiastic reply from the representative of the king who explains the legal function of the position meant to protect the interests of Sicily and make the government "hear the voice of this lovely country which is only now coming into sight of the modern world, with so many wounds to heal, so many just desires to be granted." Unimpressed by the attractive picture painted by the Chevalley, the Prince goes on to depict what he sees as the reality of the Sicilian scene:

> "We Sicilians have become accustomed, by a long, a very long hegemony of rulers who were not of our religion and who did not speak our language, to split hairs. If we had not done so we'd never have coped with Byzantine tax gatherers,

with Berber Emirs, with Spanish Viceroys. Now the bent is endemic...In Sicily it doesn't matter whether things are done well or done badly; the sin which we Sicilians never forgive is simply that of 'doing' at all. We are old, Chevalley, very old. For more than twenty-five centuries we've been bearing the weight of a superb and heterogeneous civilization, all from outside, none made by ourselves, none that we could call our own. We're as white as you are, Chevalley, and as the Queen of England; and yet for two thousand and five hundred years we've been a colony. I don't say that in complaint; it's our own fault. But even so we're worn out and exhausted."

What the Prince is pointing out to the Chevalley is the time lag in Sicilian history that makes the island's resistance to change out of step with the rest of Europe. The Prince qualifies the Sicilian phenomenon as an irremediable penchant "for voluptuous immobility, that is, for death again, our meditative air is that of a void wanting to scrutinize the enigmas of nirvana...that is the cause of the well-known time lag of a century in our artistic and intellectual life; novelties attract us only when they are dead." [28]

Lampedusa's analysis of Sicilian immutability fits in well with Santo Mazzarino's definition of the phenomenon as "history slowed down" or Giovanni Cucinotta's appraisal of the static mood that psychologically became translated into a conviction of the immutability of things and of life. The Chevalley feels disheartened by Sicilian reluctance to abandon the past. The Prince's personal suggestion for a Sicilian representative in the Italian Senate comes sudden and unexpected. His choice is Don Calogero Sedara who has "more than what you call prestige, he has power...He is the man for you. But you must be quick, as I've heard he intends to put up as candidate for the Chamber of Deputies." [29] The Chevalley, a man of exceptional integrity, had already heard distressing reports on the limitations of Don Calogero's regard for social welfare in carrying out his duties as Mayor of Donnafugata, a factor that seemed to be in striking contrast with his ability to manage the family business. Thus the Prince's unexpected suggestion is ignored. Don Calogero's ambitious plans, however, will be fulfilled ten years later when he will become senator in Rome. In his new position, he will gain the reputation of a man in touch with the demands of power, endowed with the necessary skills to surpass in wealth and in political influence the Leopards of old.

Like Verga's Mastro Don Gesualdo, Calogero Sedara marries his daughter to an impoverished aristocrat assuring a title for Angelica and her descendants and opening new doors for his ambitions. More socially evolved than Don Gesualdo, certainly more politically shrewd, he joins his lust for *la roba* to an overwhelming desire for political power. He is the new *omo de panza* ("man of substance") secure in his role of clever, wealthy politician. Whether the Prince of Salina helped Calogero Sedara fulfill his ambition by foreseeing the demise of his own class, remains an open question. He was prophetic in understanding that the shift in power–from the aristocracy to the jackals waiting to take over–is a question of time. The power of the godfathers rely on their adaptability to new political circumstances, a skill most aristocrats did not possess or did not try to develop. The *galantuomini* ("honest men") were obsequious, shrewd, and eager to change the way Sicily was run. And they did, hiding greed behind patriotic fervor while boasting respect for the law. Along with Tancredi, an unscrupulous manipulator of the historical moment, they eagerly adopted the Machiavellian refrain: "If we want things to stay as they are, things will have to change."

Predictably enough things have remained pretty much the way they were. Even today in spite of sincere efforts by many Sicilians to change the ways of the past, the Mafia's genius for adapting to different circumstances enables the *onorata società* to update its methods without altering the outcome. Like the three legs of Trinacria racing around the head of Medusa in the symbolic representation of the island, flux within immobility is an oxymoron men of respect have adopted with remarkable success.

The time in Sicilian history chosen by Luigi Pirandello, Federico De Roberto and Giuseppe di Lampedusa to examine the alternatives faced by Sicilian ruling classes after the annexation of the island to the Kingdom of Italy (1860-61) portrays a sequel of false promises and broken commitments that in many instances left the population in a worse bind than it had been under Bourbon rule. It is not until Sicily is invaded by Garibaldi's volunteers and power is transferred from the feudal lords to enterprising *galantuomini* like Don Calogero Sedara, that the *onorata società* will start replacing Sicilian ruling classes unable for the most part to guard their interests under a new political system. The Mafia, often allied with secret sects notably with the Masons as De Roberto suggests in the complex historical panorama of *I Vicerè*, took advantage of the situation merging the code of honor with the code of profit. By claiming patriotic motives and allegiance to the cause of Sicilian freedom, Mafioso feeling became a powerful force often difficult to identify because sheltered by financial and political interests that went beyond what was considered a form of insular patriotism. Eventually it became a means to secure more property and greater power. Only today, a new awakening to the Mafioso influence in the politics of the island seems to generate a concerned response among Sicilians, especially the young. The attitude is commendable but as of now too uneven to claim full results.

VI

The Defeat of Reason: Sciascia and Power

Leonardo Sciascia (1921-89) leaves behind a literary inheritance as paradoxical as the political plots he sought to expose while retaining a stubborn allegiance to the dictates of reason predicated by the French Enlightenment. His faith in reason as an unfailing guide in human behavior made him a maverick and a lasting center of controversy. The skepticism he nourished toward the dysfunctional Italian state reached its zenith in 1978 when he witnessed the government's cowardly reaction to the abduction and murder of Aldo Moro, President of the Christian Democrats' National Council. Although Moro was a victim of the Brigate Rosse (Red Brigades), then at the height of their power, Sciascia felt the hesitant behavior of the government made Moro a pawn in the hands of his abductors who executed him claiming he had been found guilty by a people court of law. As Sciascia relates in *The Moro Affair* nine weeks after the murder had taken place, the Red Brigades [1] informed anyone willing to look that the body of the victim could be found inside the trunk of a Renault parked in Via Caetani, a central street in Rome strategically located between the headquarters of the Christian Democratic Party and those of the Communist Party. As for Moro he was primarily a victim of political manipulation, or perhaps more pointedly, a scapegoat for government inefficiency and official double talk aimed to hide a pattern of intrigue complex enough to elicit the admiration of the cleverest writer of mystery stories, Sciascia being the most skilled among them. Enforcers of law and order were united in a conspiracy of silence that eventually led to the death of the doomed captive. The way Sciascia saw it, Moro became a martyr to the Italian state's unwillingness to act. The acceptance of the inevitable end that marked the Senator's last days of captivity conferred him a dignity and a consistency that–still according to Sciascia–he never possessed before. The conspiracy that led the government to become a silent partner to the murder proved that Sciascia's unrelenting criticism of Italy's business-as-usual attitude in moments of crisis was more than justified. To make the situation even worse, Milan's influential daily *Corriere della Sera* went so far as to praise Moro's act of acceptance and resignation when confronted with death, a claim altogether preposterous considering that Moro's destiny at the time had not been decided.

As one of Italy's leading intellectuals perennially engaged in political skirmishes, Sciascia could not avoid releasing a statement. He did so by publishing *The Moro Affair*. As Adrian Lyttleton pointed out [2] *The Moro Affair*, published in Palermo in 1978, was a kind of posthumous tribute to a politician whose compromising deal-making policies Sciascia had never endorsed. Whereas for most commentators the true Moro ceased to exist once he had been kidnapped, Sciascia discovered in the man fighting for his life coherence and lucidity he had not previously suspected. As can be expected, the high command of the Mafia was involved in the negotiations, this time as a possible intermediary for the floundering Italian government. *Pentito* Francesco Mannoia questioned by the FBI in 1978 was the first to relate that *Cosa Nostra* had been asked by the Italian government to intercede with the Red Brigades in order to obtain the release of the hostage. The *Cupola* (the Mafia's highest branch of government) convened and reached what could best be described as a contradictory verdict. Don Stefano Bontate and friends whose interests leaned toward the *Democrazia Cristiana*, were in favor of dealing with the abductors but the Corleonesi, led by Don Pippo Calò, were adamant in their refusal to intervene. As Judge Falcone relates, according to Mannoia *Cosa Nostra* delivered its answer to Rome in its usual cryptic fashion: "Political decisions are their thing—not our thing." [3] Don Masino Buscetta, in his confrontation with former Senator Andreotti during his deposition in Padua's trial of *Cosa Nostra'*s activities (1996) offered his version of the secret exchanges between men of honor and the government. He explained that he received a call for help from two separate sources: the Mafia and Milan's underworld. Both sides claimed to be on a humanitarian mission. However, Don Pippo Calò, reputed to be the Ambassador of *Cosa Nostra* in Rome, informed him that many influential Christian Democrats did not want Moro alive. Abandoned by the representatives of his own party, Moro was destined to become a martyr.

Sciascia's view of his own work makes his approach to the government's scandalous handling of Moro's fate a validation of his irreverent, tireless probing of the nature of power. In the 1967 preface to publisher Adelphi's reprint of his first literary success, *Parrocchie di Regalpetra* (1956), a recollection of his early years in Racalmuto, Sicily, Sciascia quotes an anonymous critic who wrote that the autobiographical story of his youth possessed all the elements that appeared in his later work. The critic added that in all probability, Sciascia was one of those writers who in their lifetime write the same book over and over again. Sciascia agreed. He faulted the critic, however, for his inability to see that his first book included a *retroterra culturale* ("cultural hinterland") that could and did generate material to be further excavated from his repository of memories. He concluded:

> "In fact all my books are one. A book about Sicily that touches upon the high lights of the past and of the present and becomes the articulation of a history where reason is always defeated and the history of those who in this defeat have been personally swept away and annihilated" (1976).[4]

Even today Sciascia's views remain controversial. His incandescent honesty, his genuine distrust for the corruption present in established power led him to take an active part in politics and to argue, mostly in vain, against a system that refused to change methods and find a way to protect its citizens from injustice. He was moved by a genuine love for truth, even though there were times when his dismayed friends, who were trying to sort out *Cosa Nostra*'s political influence on local decisions, had no choice but strongly disagree with his unfounded accusations against dedicated antagonists of the Mafia.

In 1977 Sciascia became a member of the Consiglio Comunale di Palermo, Palermo's Administrative Council. He resigned few months later stating that his aim had not been to start a political career, but to be able "to accomplish something." Since he found there was nothing to accomplish, he quit. On leaving his post, Sciascia accused the local administration of abusive behavior toward the Mafia. The methods and accusations of the anti-Mafia were, in his view, as detestable as the methods of the *onorata società*. The trial for the murders of Giuseppe Montana and Antonino Cassarà, the former chief of a military detachment called to capture an estimated eight hundred Mafiosi in hiding, the later *vice capo* of Palermo's Squadra Mobile (1985), brought convictions against people falsely accused who eventually had to be released for lack of evidence. Instead of defending the victims and condemning the miscarriage of justice, the press blasted the judge for absolving them. Sciascia cried foul. To the surprise of many Palermitani and of well-known godfathers delighted by the sudden reversal of the situation, in an article published in Milan's *Corriere della Sera* (10 January 1987) Sciascia declared himself fed up with judges who indicted innocent people by relying on their position of power. His declaration, unquestionably prompted by a sense of justice, boosted the Mafia's self-respect and gave it hope for future compromises with the law. As for Sciascia, he went as far as to call government appointed prosecutors *professionisti dell'antimafia* ("professionals of the antimafia"). In an interview with *L'Espresso* (25 January 1987) Antonino Sorgi, a good friend of Sciascia defended the dismay the writer felt when faced with the facile assumption of the justice system ready to find ties with the Mafia in every indicted individual even when the accused was proven innocent. Sorgi was fair enough to recognize "such are the problems of the anti-Mafia." However he added:

"Once this is said...I agree that perhaps my friend Sciascia should have been more specific in making his charges [against the judges]. Perhaps he has failed the obligation to be accurate and to back his views with documentation. The accusations he has made against Orlando [mayor of Palermo] and Borsellino [judge victim of the Mafia in 1992] seem to me completely unjustified."

The same issue of *L'Espresso* published an article by Nello Ajello on Sciascia's condemnation of political intrigue, "A Writer Without Illusions." Here Ajello quotes a statement made by Sciascia in an article written in the summer of 1977 nearly a year before the murder of Aldo Moro: "The State is a Ghost." Ajello contends the skepticism that the author of *The Day of the Owl* professes for the Italian government is total, unrelenting. It does not concern only the state's inability to fight the Mafia and other forms of organized crime but, and above all, its lack of credibility that inhibits the servants of the state and forbids them to carry out their duty with positive results. According to Sciascia, the State's inefficient performance and its guilty conscience merge in an inseparable, indistinguishable tangle. It should be added that this indistinguishable tangle is the same that affects the lives of Sicilian citizens who have been subject for centuries to political abuses and unrelenting poverty.

Leonardo Sciascia learned his first lesson on poverty while growing up in Racalmuto near Agrigento, Luigi Pirandello's hometown, the grandson of an employee of the *zolfare* (sulphur mines) where workers were underpaid and without hope for betterment. Other sources of employment in the zone were the *saline* (salt flats), where the pay and treatment of the workers were even worse. Leonardo's family was not as economically deprived as most families in Racalmuto where the children grew up cold, hungry, without decent clothes and understandably uninterested in getting an education. Their instinct for survival made them concentrate on food, clothes, warmth in winter and other needs the Fascists and the parties that followed them after WW II failed to provide. Sciascia, a committed schoolteacher, empathized with the children victims of a system unfit for animals. The Catholic Church's pity was limited to the observance of the ritual without consideration for the hardships faced by the people. The poor were born poor, lived poor and died poor. Changes were not expected nor deemed necessary by the authorities. After WW II political candidates (Christian Democrats, Neo-Fascists, Monarchist, Communists) made their platform a success by using grandiloquence to make promises they never kept.

The Mafia, silenced by Fascist persecution, emerged more powerful than ever, helped in its recovery by the AMG (American Military Government) grateful to the "men of honor" for their generous help during the invasion of Sicily. The Mafia became enshrined in the system by using the excuse that its resistance to Fascism and the persecutions it had suffered under Cesare Mori, *Il Prefetto di Ferro* ("The Iron Prefect"), Mussolini's envoy to Sicily, had been caused by its unshakable faith in democracy. The Allies at first believed such claims, but eventually they discovered that the patriotic fervor displayed by Mafiosi did not stop them from killing, stealing and conducting business as usual in the best interest of the family. Sciascia saw all this very clearly, never underestimating the hypocrisy of the *galantuomini*, ironically meaning 'honest men,' and their ability to use the needy eager to improve their economic status to achieve their end. He found the inefficiency and double standard of the Italian government even more damnable. His faith in reason as an unfailing guide in human behavior made him a lasting center of controversy. A confirmed enemy of Mafia criminality, Sciascia was too Sicilian to deny the deep, undeniable roots that makes the *onorata società* an integral part of the history of the island. Possessions, be it land ownership, construction, bank transactions or political power generates struggles that call for the removal of obstacles—mostly human lives. A network of invisible links spins its web: silent, ominous, and admirably efficient. Tradition and history are on its side. There is not a government attempt to upset its plans and even if there might be, the *onorata società* recognizes only its own government. As previously pointed out, the legislative intricacies of *Cosa Nostra* were born from a tradition where oppression and death lived in congenial symbiosis, the latter functioning as a source of strength in defying the law. Sciascia–similar in this to his Agrigentino predecessor Luigi Pirandello–saw the irony of this ingrained attitude. He analyzed the unique logic of Mafia power, dissected it, searched its most recondite motivation and found all efforts, legal or literary, to dismantle its network of intrigue quite useless. The situations he plotted in his stories became increasingly complex and, as a consequence, more evasive. Eventually they became conspiracies impossible to penetrate. It was a way for Sciascia to point out similar situations in the government where Mafia and influential members of Parliament became allies ready to protect their interests at all costs as Senator Moro's abduction and execution demonstrated.

Leonardo Sciascia has left an impressive collection of novels, essays, short stories, plays, among these, as already pointed out, his adaptation of *I Mafiusi di la Vicaria di Palermu* to contemporary implications of Mafia political power. Sciascia displays a peculiar attraction-revulsion to the world of *omertà* stemming perhaps from his personal identification with *sentire Mafioso*, the way Sicilians think and feel. Sciascia's fiery imagination is tempered by a cold, lucid appraisal of the breaking point when reason withdraws and instinct reaches the fatal point of no return. Existence, Sciascia implies, is a puzzle where eagerly sought solutions can lead to the threshold of death. Claude Ambroise in "Les Traces de Vie" points out that Sciascia combines two questions essential to the good mystery writer: "Who has killed him?" and "Why death?" While the first question can be answered, the second remains without reply. The reason is not hard to find. The moment of truth is shrouded in lasting *omertà*. Sciascia's intellectual kinship with Pirandello helps decipher basic tenets that set his detective fiction apart. The two writers' common denominator is the rapport they establish between reality and appearance or, even more pointedly, the perception of the absurd that makes so many of their characters renege what they have endorsed all along: reasonable behavior. The Pirandellian anti-hero driven by an overwhelming urge to defy society reflects the image of the exploited Sicilian citizen catapulted into a world where the usual concept of justice does not function. Sciascia identifies with Pirandello's approach to reality because he recognizes that what Italians living in the peninsula may find outrageous behavior, in Sicily is not only acceptable but also quite ordinary. His writing reflects the struggle between an intense emotional turmoil and a rational scrutiny indispensable if one is to decide what is the most expedient means to achieve the wanted result. To survive, flexibility is a must, a factor never ignored by Sciascia who makes his men of honor take Machiavelli to heart by showing remarkable adaptability to changing times. This, however, is not always true of Sciascia's heroes who do not heed the warnings of reason and follow their deadly leads to the end. Their cleverness makes them worthy opponents of the godfathers who may admire their courage but cannot allow them to interfere in the family business. Although Sciascia's fiction never looses sight of *Cosa Nostra*'s intrigues, he makes sure that the undercover operations of the *onorata società* mingle with equally damnable governmental schemes such as he witnessed in a stormy political career that culminated in his being appointed to the European Parliament where, predictably enough, he resigned disgusted by debates leading nowhere.

Sciascia remains unique insofar as his intuitions go further than those of a writer who has intimate knowledge of his material. They include the insights of a Sicilian who nourishes a deep love–at times perverse–for *l'isola del sole* ("the island of the sun") as novelist Luigi Capuana referred to Sicily, an island where the sun-flooded landscape presents a disconcerting amalgam of fertile groves, dirt cracked by the heat, caves gaping from inaccessible rocks, ruins left by Greeks, Arabs, Romans, Normans, Spaniards, and all those who contributed to make Trinacria the *memento mori* (loosely translated "remember you are going to die") of assorted Mediterranean civilizations.

Sciascia's fiction is a lot more than an absorbing story. He uses literature to challenge the reader through unsuspected allusions that enrich the text and add tension to the narrative. He engages in an intriguing game using semantic metamorphoses that allow officers of the law to become the alter ego of the Mafiosi they are after. The Mafia syndrome in Sciascia's narrative reaches its highest points with his early novel, *Il giorno della civetta* ("The Day of the Owl"). The story relies on a series of sharply drawn sketches located for the most part in an unspecified provincial town near Palermo. The opening event–the murder of Salvatore Colasberna, an independent and fairly honest construction contractor–allows Sciascia to introduce several conversations among Sicilian political representatives in Rome. These anonymous speakers are distinguished only by physical traits reminiscent of their various ancestries–Arab, Norman, Spanish–or by impressive political titles such as "Minister," or "Excellency," fulfilling the double purpose of indicating their position in the government and of satirizing Italian fondness for redundant titles. At the time the book was published (1961), the problem of Mafia controlled *appalti* ("construction monopolies") had become one of the leading issues on the island. Even today the countryside near Palermo is scarred with buildings left unfinished because of improper handling of funds. Reticent Sicilians explain the phenomenon as lack of payments by emigrants who planned to return and settle here while others more willing to disregard the code of silence in favor of the truth, volunteer that the government because of illicit gains by Mafia contractors stopped the projects. Whatever the case, the construction industry has been powerfully affected by *Cosa Nostra* thus the case made by Sciascia in the novel relates with impressive immediacy the saga of the *appalti*, the building fever that scarred the island's garden area from Palermo to Bagheria with a barrage of ugly, often unsafe building projects.

The Day of the Owl starts with one of the cleverest murder scenes in the mystery genre. Early one morning as independent contractor Salvatore Colasberna is about to board the bus for Palermo in the local piazza, he is killed with two shots of *lupara* (a particular gun used by the Mafia) coming from direction unknown and predictably ignored by those present who insist they had not seen the murderer. The reason? They were not there. A man selling fritters stationed two paces from the bus is just in time to remove himself and his merchandise from the suspicious location but is spotted by a policeman, Carabiniere Sposito, who has started to investigate the circumstances of the murder. The questioning ends with a classic instance of *omertà*: "I want to know only one thing, and, if you tell me, you can go off at once and sell your fritters to the kids: who fired the shots?" "Why," asked the fritter-seller, astonished and inquisitive, "has there been a shooting?" [5] Never missing the opportunity to call the attention of the reader to amusing coincidences, Sciascia points out that the two streets meeting at the corner where the fatal shots had been fired are named Via Cavour and Piazza Garibaldi, timely reminders of Prime Minister Camillo Benso Count of Cavour who engineered Sicily's reunion with the Italian mainland and

Giuseppe Garibaldi, the celebrated general whose landing in Sicily brought Cavour's plans to fruition.

At the police station, the two surviving Colasberna brothers arrive dressed in black according to the local custom, ashamed to be in such a location but mostly annoyed to be kept waiting by an unknown police officer. They ponder the insult they have received when Captain Bellodi, the Chief of Police, an ex-partisan in World War II, arrives young, tall and fair skinned speaking with an accent that gives him away as a mainlander from northern Italy. Throughout the story Sciascia places Captain Bellodi in the difficult role of a well read, enlightened police officer bent on exposing the roots of Mafia evil yet ready to justify its existence when necessary to expose the unholy alliance between criminality and government.

The situation at the police station becomes even more complex when the wife of Paolo Nicolosi, a tree-trimmer by trade, arrives to denounce her husband's five days disappearance. Since in Sicily this is taken as factual proof that the missing party is *morto ammazzato* ("dead murdered") everyone starts speaking of him in the past tense referring to his wife as "the widow," offering an admirable example of linguistic adaptability to unexpected events. Captain Bellodi addresses his questions in a calm, polite manner quite natural to him but also meant to defuse Sicilian distrust of authority. As can be expected he gets nowhere, still, he follows the few leads with exceptional coherence sharing insights into Sicilian history and literature while inserting in the narrative clues for any reader willing to play a game of philological anagrams.

Sciascia has often claimed that literature must function as an encyclopedia where intertextual references enrich the text through historical and literary connotations even though these connotations are not essential to the understanding of the plot. By peculiar coincidence this approach works well with the Mafia. The reluctance of men of honor to use words to relate a message and their use of eye contact to communicate with others who share *il medesimo sentire* ("the same feeling") becomes a stylistic device curiously attuned to trends in twentieth-century literature and, in the case of Sciascia, legitimized by a tradition that goes well beyond the demands of literary conventions. The following anecdote illustrates the point. In January 1996 during hearings held in Padua to indict appointee senator for life Giulio Andreotti for his involvement in the Moro conspiracy, Saverio Lodato, Sicilian envoy for the Communist daily *L'Unità*, spent some time with Don Masino Buscetta, Italy's leading man of honor who was a major witness in the trial. Lodato relates how hard it was for Buscetta to say what he meant. His speech was replete with sloppy language, grammatical errors, and inappropriate syntax. After stating that Buscetta was one of the last great leaders of a criminal organization that had centuries of tradition behind it, Lodato points out that members of the Mafia had been accustomed to communicate through silence and eye contact developing an uncanny ability to shun the use of words. Under the circumstances Buscetta was forced to use a language totally unfamiliar to him. In short he was lending his voice to explain an organization that had always despised the use of words. As he told Lodato, he was haunted by the possibility of revealing secrets he did not want to divulge.[6] Brevity and lexical conventions known only to the Mafioso is the key in communicating with other members bound by the same pledge of *omertà*.

In an interview Sciascia gave to Jean Noel Schifano, a feature writer for the French journal *L'Arc*, he stated: "Je joue toujours avec les titres et avec les citations" "I always play with titles and quotations," a perplexing invitation to find hidden meanings especially applicable to *The Day of the Owl* where glancing at history through anagrams concealed in the text, helps understand why the Mafia exists and goes on existing without signs of abating. Sciascia had the advantage of feeling and thinking like a Mafioso without being one. In *Venti Anni di Mafia* (*Twenty Years of Mafia*), Saverio Lodato relates a conversation he had with judges Giovanni Falcone and Paolo Borsellino shortly before they were murdered. Both agreed that in their youth, long before becoming prosecutors, they had learned what the Mafia was like by reading *The Day of the Owl*, the best example of Sciascia's exceptional insight into Mafioso ways. The novel details various viewpoints intended to expose the contagious disease that afflicts the highest echelons of the Italian government. Several conversations in Rome among anonymous Sicilian members of Parliament present a counterpoint to Captain Bellodi's investigation to expose Colasberna's murderers. These anonymous exchanges, only marginally related to the development of the story, function as a Greek chorus that offers readers an insight into corrupted Mafia practices and political intrigue. This practice facilitates the exploitation of workers and is often used by the Mafia–an association conservative to a fault–to protect family interests from labor interferences that can be damaging to its many enterprises. What goes on in Italy is a reversal of the *Cosa Nostra* pay-offs that have plagued New York's unions for years, it is also a confirmation of Mafia flexibility and offers further evidence that expediency and adaptability to local needs are the organization's best assurance of survival.

In an exchange between a man addressed as His Excellency and another Excellency, this one nameless, the first speaker voices concern over Colasberna's murder as he wonders if the Minister, anonymous as well, is aware of the grave situation in Sicily. He promptly classifies Captain Bellodi as a Communist although his interlocutor insists that Bellodi is a Socialist—a party distinction His Excellency refuses to make. Still, in order to remove the crown of martyrdom from the extinct Colasberna, a motive for the murder must be found. What could be better than a vendetta for adultery or something of the kind? His interlocutor, not a Sicilian, annoyed by the simplistic solution insists that it is clearly a Mafia crime. The problem, still according to His Excellency, is that Bellodi has a fixation about the Mafia. One of those Northerners with the head full of prejudices who begin to see the Mafia in everything before they even gets off the ferryboat. In conclusion, if the public believes that Colasberna has been murdered by the Mafia, as some papers insist he has, "we are sunk." The skirmish between the two ends in a question His Excellency poses to his reluctant listener: "Do you believe in the Mafia?' The man hesitates: "Well, er... And you?" "No. I don't." His Excellency goes on:

> "We two [himself and the absent Minister] both Sicilians, don't believe in the Mafia. That ought to mean something to you, who evidently do. But I can understand you. You aren't Sicilian and prejudices die hard."[7]

Prejudices or not, Captain Bellodi knows he is in a bind. People are scared to talk. Fear of the police outranks fear of the Mafia. Its presence, after all, has been part of the local scene from time immemorial. Recollections of police brutality committed during the regime of Cesare Mori, Mussolini's appointee, are still with them and Bellodi's polite, low-key manner does not erase the fear instilled by centuries of cruelties perpetrated by feudal lords, greedy barons, French sovereigns, Spanish Vicerè, Fascist police and established authority in general. Back in Rome influential members of the government are investigating the possibility of doing away with Bellodi and his effective handling of the Colasberna murder.

Sciascia does not miss the opportunity to interpolate Sicilian sensuality with political maneuvers meant to retain influence and, more importantly, the wealth accumulated through land acquisitions and property rights. During a conversation in a Roman cafe between "a man in black"–a reference to Spanish traditional attire–and "a fair man"–a Sicilian of Norman descent–whose thinking was as similar as they "differed...in physique and manner" Sciascia draws a convincing picture of Sicilian realities. The fair man and the dark man are equally charmed by a svelte cloakroom girl in a snugly fitted dress that, in their active imagination, should be removed stitch by stitch. While their eyes wander and their imagination proceeds to peel off the girl's attire, their minds are elsewhere. The thorn in their side is Captain Bellodi, who has declared war on local contractors. One of the speakers increasingly irritated by what he considers to be the audacity of Bellodi relates how this political upstart had taken the side of the sulfur miners looking for better working conditions against the rightful owner of the mines–namely himself–a man of principles and a good Catholic. He fervently hopes that with the help of a friend who has connections where connections count, there will be a way to send Bellodi back home to eat polenta, yellow corn-mush.

On the Sicilian front Bellodi starts pulling together the strings of his recalcitrant puppets. What gives the investigation a badly needed turn is the unexpected revelation of the local informer, Calogero Dibella known as *Parrinieddu* or Little Priest—a sarcastic reference to his confessional habits of attentive listener to other people's secrets. This time, however, the Little Priest has mailed the Captain the name of the powerful godfather who has ordered Colasberna's murder. He is aware that his decision will cost him his life and, paralyzed by fear, he waits for the *lupara* (a particular gun used by the Mafia) to shoot him. The end comes as he reaches the door of his house. Captain Bellodi receives the letter when Parrinieddu is already dead. The Captain's reaction is telling:

> "By his death, his last farewell, the informer had come into a closer, more human relationship; this might be unpleasant, vexatious; but in the feelings and thoughts of the man who shared them they brought a response of sympathy, of spiritual sympathy."

It is not only "spiritual sympathy" between the two, it is a kinship brought on by a similarity of vocations. A policeman is a spy for the law and an informer is a spy for the Mafia. They are intimately bound by a legacy of historical wrongdoings. Sciascia ironically ties them together using a juxtaposition of names connected to a reference in Roman history. Thus Dibella (Di-bella) the Mafioso informer, and Bellodi (Bello-di) the policeman, have surnames suggestive of the *De Bello Gallico*, Julius Caesar's memoirs of his bloody campaign against the Gauls who had rebelled against Roman rule. Caesar reasserted sovereignty over the insurgent populations, enabling Rome to continue its repressive policies by seizing the resources of conquered lands to fill its coffers and granaries, a fate Sicily had endured since Roman conquest in 210 B.C.

Calogero Dibella's last moments focus on the terrifying imagery of the prey escaping the aggressor aware at every turn of the uselessness of its efforts. He is constantly depicted "with a mastiff at his heels" afraid "to be shot down like a dog" terrified by what he envisions as his unforgivable treason of omertà "his body...a terror soaked sponge." The image of death as a porous trap holding the culprit in a last embrace prepares the reader for the discovery of the body of Nicolosi, the tree trimmer, at the bottom of the *chiarchiaro* ("a stony place") of Gramoli "a huge black-holed sponge soaking up the light flooding the landscape" that makes Captain Bellodi think of it as the place "where God throws in the sponge." The association with death becomes even more precise as the sergeant accompanying Bellodi quotes a popular saying: "E lu cuccu ci dissi a li cuccuotti: A lu chiarchiaru nni vidiemmu tutti ("An owl told his owlets: we'll all meet in the end at the chiarchiaro"). No one seems quite sure why the *chiarchiaro* had become associated with death. At this juncture, however, the body at the bottom of the thirty-foot shaft justifies the association. As a peasant volunteers to tie the victim to a rope and bring him up, the dog imagery used to describe the mastiff metaphorically gnawing Dibella's stomach becomes associated with momentous religious and political symbolism.

While waiting for the recovery of the body, Captain Bellodi wanders to a nearby farm house where he is met by a handsome brown mongrel with little violet half-moons over its yellow eyes by the name of Barruggieddu. According to its owner the dog has the tendency to bite anyone who tries to pet him. Captain Bellodi, who has more than a passing interest in philology, asks the reason for the unusual name. The dog owner explains that maybe the right name was Barricieddu or maybe Bargieddu. Regardless of its origin the name was a feared reminder of *Bargello*, the evil officer in a position of command. Bellodi's mind, trained in historical-theological parallelisms, reverts to the Dominicans who ruled the Inquisition, "a word that conjured up a dark empty crypt and stirred gloomy echoes of history." Since the Dominicans were known as *Domini Canes* or Hounds of the Lord, Sciascia's penchant for caustic associations unites the Dominicans, responsible for the horrors of the Inquisition with the policeman or *bargello* persecuting innocent people and makes the dog eager to bite a friendly hand, a symbol of treachery. The reference sheds light on the complex historical situation that for centuries has engendered the need for secrecy and protection that could be afforded only by an extended family sharing the same secrecy, the same rapport of mutual trust–*amici degli amici*–in short a society of ("friends of friends"). Solidarity and silence conceived at first as a necessary shield to protect the family's secret ventures eventually would degenerate into criminal alliances ruled by deceit and murder.

Still it is in the title of the story, *The Day of the Owl*, that the parable reveals its true meaning. In his afterward to the English translation of the novel Frank Kermode has solved the puzzle of the story's caption by suggesting Shakespeare's Henry VI Part III, as Sciascia's intentional source. He writes:

"The title is derived from some lines in Shakespeare's Henry VI

> And he that will not fight for such a hope
> Go home to bed, and like the owl by day
> If he arise, be mocked and wondered at.
> [5.4.55]

The speaker is Somerset, and it may be worth noting that a couple of scenes later we see him defeated and led off to execution. Yet the point seems to be that it is more absurd not to fight than to fight for justice, however slight the chance of victory."[8]

Something else could be added to Kermode's insightful comment. In structuring the book, Sciascia uses a system of concatenation linked by a series of brief tableaux the reader must assemble into a meaningful whole. This system reflects the pattern of Shakespeare's early histories where the intricate action, the execution of murders, the alternate momentum of winning or losing battles are seen as a pageant unfolding before the eyes of the spectators in brief scenes linked to ulterior developments through transitions the viewer of the play–in this case the reader–must assemble without losing sight of the various narrative links. Henry VI, Part III, has the effect of a checker match: every move implies the elimination of a rival, the game, however, goes on ad infinitum without a solution in sight as every conquest foretells a bloody reversal. In the checkerboard of history, as in the fierce rivalry of Mafia *cosche* ("clan"), there is no such thing as a lasting victory. The players in this game of hazard are constantly urged to go on by greed and by political gain. As the owl by day represents an inversion in the order of nature, the betrayal of laws stipulated to guarantee the common good spells the end of a civilized society.

Acknowledged as one of Shakespeare's most pessimistic histories, Henry VI portrays the unending evils of civil war and reciprocal betrayal. Richard, the future Richard III, plots to murder King Edward and his son, the Prince of Wales. Family murder begets family murder and hatred instigated by the wish to increase land holdings and power erodes all civilized restraint engendering even greater destruction. Common denominators in the drama are bloody competition and the resolve to keep on fighting, establishing in Sciascia's mind a link with the struggle of powerful Mafia families always engaged in eliminating each other.

While in preceding histories Shakespeare presents the events as scenes from history, here the primary theme becomes moral order. Those who commit crimes against divine justice and mercy may flourish for a time, but eventually are destroyed. In the complex background of the War of the Roses, the last hope of Lancaster and his followers are destroyed in the battle of Tewkesbury (May 4, 1471). Queen Margaret and her son, the young Prince of Wales, are captured and the boy is slain before her eyes by King Edward and his brothers. Before the bloody deed takes place, Oxford, who is soon to be killed, expresses his appreciation for the courage of the youthful Prince of Wales. Addressing himself to Queen Margaret who, incidentally, is heiress to Sicily, and to her son he praises them both:

> Women and children of so high a courage,
> And warriors faint? Why, it were perpetual shame.
> O brave young prince! Thy famous grandfather
> Doth live again in thee. Long mayst thou live
> To bare his image and renew his glories.
> [5.4.50-54]

Somerset, an ally to the queen, adds the well known words designed to express his spite for anyone who indulges in unnatural behavior by making the comparison with an owl who, failing to sleep in the day and to fly at night, as it was destined to do, inverts the order of nature and, as a result, "is mocked and wondered at." Shakespeare knows thirst for power will not stop Richard and his accomplices from stabbing to death the young heir to the throne, disrupting once more the moral order of the kingdom. Hunger for power makes the end justify the means, turns day into night, and negates the natural attributes of the owl by turning it into a day bird. Sciascia suggests that the Mafia, blinded by its mirage of possessions and power, ignores all boundaries of civilized behavior preying on its victims in a merciless series of *vendette trasversali* ("vengeances across the line") like a bird of prey that no longer respects the natural order and becomes a harbinger of death.

The final confrontation between Captain Bellodi and the ruling godfather, Don Mariano Arena, a man without formal education equipped, however, with exceptional intelligence and an abundant reserve of *sentire Mafioso* offers a peculiar turn in the narrative leaving the reader with more questions than answers. Don Mariano Arena emerges as a posthumous heir to the island's celebrated oratorical tradition–his speech carefully thought out and admirably delivered–argues a wisdom that demands respect. When Bellodi asks him if he had connections with Calogero Dibella the murdered informer also known as Parrinieddu, his immediate concern is to qualify the nature of the question according to the strictest rules of rhetoric. "Did the inspector mean: simple acquaintance, friendship or common interests?" Knowing he is faced with an exceptional antagonist, Bellodi questions Don Mariano about the sources of his impressive and unexplainable income. Bellodi's research on the relevant amounts is impeccably correct. He nearly enrages the cool headed Don when he mentions the cost of his daughter's education in a finishing school in Lausanne, where she is becoming refined and perhaps a bit estranged from her father's questionable procedures. Proud and self-assured Don Mariano rebuffs: "My daughter is like me." The next topic of conversation deals with income-tax evasion, but Don Mariano is not disturbed by Bellodi's carefully researched evidence nor by his statement that in other parts of the world eluding taxes is considered a crime of major proportions. The conversation proceeds with uneven results till Don Mariano delivers what has become one of the most famous quotes in the literature of the Mafia:

> "I...have a certain experience of the world and what we call humanity–all hot air that word–I divide into five categories: men, half-men, pigmies, arse-crawlers–if you'll excuse the expression–and quackers. Men are very few indeed; half-men few, and I'd be content if humanity finished with them...But no, it sinks even lower, to the pigmies who're like children trying to be grown-ups, monkeys going through the motions of their elders...Then down even lower we go, to the arse-crowlers who're legion...And finally to the quackers; they ought to just exist, like ducks in a pond: their

lives have no more point or meaning...But you, even if you nail me to these documents like Christ to His Cross, you're a man."

"So are you," said the captain, not without emotion. Bellodi immediately repents of his emotional outburst yet the qualification of *omo* ("man") bestowed by a powerful godfather intensifies the uneasiness of his feelings already caught between antagonism and admiration. This factor will eventually lead him to seek another assignment in Sicily, in spite of the knowledge that in returning to the island he is probably signing his own death warrant.

The conversation continues through uncharted paths leading to philosophy and religion. Bellodi asks Don Mariano if he has read the Gospel. A true man of honor, Don Mariano admits his knowledge of the Gospel is limited. Actually what he knows he has learned from listening to the priest on Sunday. He goes as far as to express his admiration for the message of Christ but mostly for the splendid decor of Catholic churches as he proclaims: "The Church is all beautiful." Bellodi retorts: "For you, I see, beauty has nothing to do with truth." But the reply comes quickly: "Truth is at the bottom of a well: look into it and you see the sun and the moon; but if you throw yourself in it, there's no more sun or moon: just truth." Bellodi retorts: "You have helped many a man to find truth at the bottom of a well." Don Mariano knows he is losing ground, but defends himself, confident as usual that his friends in Rome will manage to prove the northern intruder completely off the mark, relieve him of the investigation and assure building contractors like him a continued, profitable collaboration with the government.

Leaving the Romans to their political intrigues and the Sicilians to run the family business, Sciascia returns to Captain Bellodi by now on sick leave in his home town of Parma where he is recuperating from what a physician friend diagnoses as "sign of liver trouble" thus establishing a further link between Bellodi, the policeman, and his professional alter-ego Calogero Dibella, the murdered informer who was overly fond of Averna's bitter vermouth and suffered from cirrhosis of the liver.[9] To make matters even worse Bellodi reads in the newspapers that his case against Don Mariano Arena has been dismantled piece by piece since "the patient web of clues woven by the captain and the Public Prosecutor has melted into thin air." The only positive sign left for Bellodi is Don Mariano Arena referring to him as "a man" in his frequent interviews with the media, a compliment that, considering the source, has the effect of pleasing and irritating him at the same time. To a journalist who asks him to clarify what kind of man Bellodi is, Don Mariano replies angrily that definitions are not necessary since "if I say the Captain is a man, he's a man and that's all there is to it." The reply makes Bellodi think of a victorious general praising a defeated adversary—a thought that in all probability would have pleased Don Mariano.

Once more Verga's Don Gesualdo's greed for land and property dominates the scene. Unscrupulous profits mark the end of effective government controls on crimes too often tied to political and financial interests. In a way *The Day of the Owl* describes circumstances similar to *The Moro Affair* before the abduction and murder of the Christian Democrat leader took place. The government's discreet alliance with the Mafia in profitable deals justifies what has been called by some Sciascia's Sicilian pessimism. Actually Sciascia has a clear vision of how *la politica del carciofo* ("the politics of the artichoke") affects the welfare of the country. Still the admiration Bellodi (Sciascia) feels for Don Mariano is genuine. The aging godfather is the relic of a time when the family was the only unit able to safeguard the interests of its members and guarantee safe transfer of *la roba* to their heirs. Bellodi brings back from Sicily disappointments and frustrations, yet he cannot resist the lure of Trinacria, the beautiful enchantress who claims his devotion and has already plotted his destruction. He has become another link in the chain that stretches from the mainland to the island like an irresistible force that cannot be rescinded. He knows he will go back "even if it is the end of me," a prophecy that brands his future with the fatal menace of the *chiarchiaro* ("a stony place") waiting for more victims.

Sciascia's mature narrative, while relying on circumstances suggesting realistic developments, remains open ended. Even his most resourceful characters become entangled in criminal plots too subtle to decipher and in many cases in conspiracies too complex to present a solution. In an ironic reversal of expected behavior Sciascia's anti-heroes occasionally are doomed by their inability to be different from the people they suspect. Some are victims of their sensual nature as they find themselves ensnared by the lure of feminine appeal that makes them fall victim of latent sensual longings subtly instigated and cleverly managed by Mafia ingenuity. Such is the case of schoolteacher Professor Laurana in *A Man's Blessing* (1966). The Italian title of the novel seems more appropriate, *A ciascuno il suo* ("To each his due"). The motto derives from the heading of Vatican City's daily newspaper *L'Osservatore Romano*: "Unicuique suum non praevalebunt," an adaptation of Roman law that states "Iustitia est unicuique suum tribune" ("Justice consists in giving each person his due"). Since such ideal form of justice does not coincide with the interests of the Mafia, the title is an ironic comment on the end of the story where everyone gets his due—unsought in the case of the protagonist.

In a preface to *A ciascuno il suo* Sciascia insists that the story–his best-known Mafia story since *The Day of the Owl*–is related not only to Sicily, but also to what he calls the "Sicilization of Italy." He also warns that the locality is not as important as it seems. What counts is the unfolding of a situation that could happen anywhere at anytime. He calls the tale a parable or an *exemplum* in the medieval sense. He regrets that the story takes place at a time when the Socialist Party–a close ally of the Communist Party he favored–was finally becoming a real presence in the Italian government. He ends by quoting Lampedusa's *The Leopard*, by now a point of reference for every frustrated Sicilian reformer: "If we want things to stay as they are, things will have to change."

As a matter of fact in *A Man's Blessings*, change is at hand in the life of the beautiful wife of Doctor Roscio, the local physician. He obviously has become an obstacle to the fulfillment of her love for her powerful Mafioso cousin who provides for the husband's lasting removal during a hunting expedition the doctor undertakes with Signor Manno, the local pharmacist, whose tragic destiny is sealed by being in the right place at the wrong time. Cut out letters from the heading of *L'Osservatore Romano*, the Vatican's official daily paper, have been used to compose the threatening message sent to the surprised pharmacist: "For what you have done, you'll die." The problem is that the pharmacist, a peaceful man dedicated to his wife, hunting, and his dogs, does not quite know what he has done to deserve to die.

In comes Professor Laurana, a well-read, timid teacher of literature who lives with his mother and feels more comfortable with books then with women. Laurana is clever enough to suspect something. He becomes the victim of a conspiracy of silence when the wife of Doctor Roscio, by now a widow seductively attired in the black finery prescribed by mourning, lures him into a deadly trap. Tricked into a rendezvous in a cafe in a nearby city, possibly Palermo, he anxiously waits for her arrival while reading the enlightened prose of his beloved Voltaire. Since it is getting late and the widow does not show up, he has no choice but to go to the station and catch the last train home. Laurana is murdered for being closer to the discovery of the assassin than anyone had suspected and his body, never to be found, is dumped in an abandoned sulphur mine similar to the *chiarchiaro* of Gramoli in *The Day of the Owl*. The widow Roscio and her Mafioso cousin can enjoy at last their well-deserved happiness legally enforced by a wedding. The tale ends with speculations of what made Professor Laurana disappear so suddenly and completely. His case is compared by the locals to what happened fifty years before to Antonio Patò during the Easter celebration of the Mortorio, a procession commemorating the death of Christ, where Patò was chosen to impersonate Judas. It seems that Patò disappeared in a hole in the ground as the tradition wanted Judas to do only that Judas-Patò never reappeared. The incident was commemorated by a popular saying: "to vanish like Antonio Patò in the Mortorio," a reference to someone never to be seen again—at least among the living. The locals agree Professor Laurana had suffered a destiny similar to Patò's and, as it happened in the case of his predecessor, omertà had sealed forever his resting place.

In *Equal Danger* (1971), *Todo Modo* (1974), and *A Straightforward Tale* (1989), Sciascia's plots become increasingly delocalized as the tentacles of the *piovra* reach in the most recondite places of public and private life. Unquestionably influenced by his negative political experiences, Sciascia sees the structure of power increasingly infected by obscure plots until the state becomes a conglomeration of interests linked through a chain of reciprocal betrayals. *Equal*

The Defeat of Reason: Sciascia and Power 117

Danger depicts a complex pattern of deceit that strikes victims engaged in a deadly gamble where the highest stake is political power. Organized crime has powerful *cadres* ("nucleus") ready to execute judges, former allies, revolutionaries and detectives gone too far in their pursuit of clues. Such is the case with Inspector Americo Rogas whose investigation of several murdered judges lead to dangerous discoveries. Corruption has infiltrated the role of justice. Coherence is absent in a paradoxical display of power that allows Narco–obvious short for narcotics–to live in a splendid baroque palace built by a cardinal at a time when the church was in charge and ruled all transactions—a privilege apparently inherited by new power groups' offshoots of the Mafia. Political expediency is the clue to the ongoing massacre of *cadaveri eccellenti* ("excellent victims") targeted by the alliance between revolutionaries and drug dealers. The chain of murders cannot be complete without the execution of Rogas who has gone too far in gathering evidence of conspiracies closely related to corruption in government. The simultaneous murders of Rogas and Amar–Secretary General of the International Revolutionary Party–in a room of the National Gallery of Art unleashes the usual investigations meant to establish the where, why, and how of the double murder. The where is obvious: Amar in Room XII under a famous portrait by Velasquez, Rogas in Room XI under the painting of the Madonna of the Chain, work of an unknown fifteenth-century Florentine painter who could not have foreseen how the series of murders executed by organized crime would bestow an esoteric meaning to the chain of his Madonna. The bodies are discovered by a terrified herd of American tourists who happen to stumble upon the grisly spectacle while visiting the museum. As the investigation proceeds without results, the daily news announces a third, even more grievous murder: the assassination of Ernest Riches, President of the Supreme Court, killed in his home as his old and faithful servant was taking a Sunday morning stroll. Taking a Sunday stroll is a practice long established in Mafia murders to remove oneself from the action.

The Center of Special Information solves the puzzle of the double murder in the Museum by informing Cusan, Rogas' closest friend, that Rogas has been eliminated by one of their undercover agents because Rogas had killed Amar and was obviously too dangerous to be alive. The explanation coming from the usual unimpeachable sources eliminates the need for further investigation. Once more reasons of state are invoked to create a useful cover up. The concatenation of murders is left without a solution with the implied suggestion that it will keep growing, adding more *cadaveri eccellenti* to an already long list. Sciascia's comments on *Equal Danger*, a story he calls "a parody," emphasize the uneasy feeling he felt in witnessing the situation he had dramatized come true in the daily stage of Italian politics. Sciascia admitted that the tale he had started as "an amusing pastime" had degenerated into "an uncomfortable fable about power anywhere in the world, about power that, in the impenetrable form of concatenation that we can roughly term Mafioso, works steadily greater degradation. Lastly, I should add that I kept this fable in a drawer in my desk for more than two years. Why? I don't know, but this could be an explanation: I began writing it with amusement, and as I was finishing it I was no longer amused."[10]

Although Sciascia does not say, he might have felt the same while writing *Todo Modo*, another parody prefaced by an excerpt from Dionysius the Aeropagite's *De Mystica Theologia*, where the Bishop of Athens explains the way to practice appropriate spiritual exercises–a system eventually adopted by Ignatius of Loyola, founder of the Jesuits, to achieve a perfect union with God. Sciascia describes a peculiar monastery, the Hermitage of Zafer (short for the Italian word *zaferano* ("saffron"), a spice reminiscent of Arab domination in Sicily) dedicated to refresh and invigorate flesh and spirit of high rank politicians and industrial magnates who find in this oasis of peace a perfect balance between body (exquisite cuisine and beautiful, discreet prostitutes) and soul (spiritual exercises under the guidance of Don Mariano, a highly cultivated Jesuit). The narrator, a successful painter on vacation, stumbles on the hermitage by chance and is reluctantly accepted by the monks as pensioner. He seizes upon his unexpected encounter with Jesuit-hotelier Don Mariano as an occasion to deepen his understanding of the activities in this peculiar clerical setting where Catholicism, industry and political power share tangential interests not always attuned to each other, as is revealed by several murders that destroy the success of the spiritual exercises. Don Mariano's murder annuls further attempts to test the meaning of the order's formula for success: "todo modo, todo modo…para buscar y hallar la voluntad divina" "this is the way, this is the way…to seek and discover the divine will." A will evidently not too favorable to the leader of the retreat or to some of the guests targeted by powerful rivals and soon turned into *cadaveri eccellenti*.

As Sciascia's fiction increasingly leans toward a surrealistic setting, Mafia and Mafiosi become an elusive presence—efficient, threatening, unfathomable. It is no longer a question of the police fighting the odds. The increasing infiltration of *Cosa Nostra* in the high echelons of government hampers efforts to eradicate the growing menace. As a result, the ability of the law to enforce and administer justice is radically weakened.

Sciascia's farewell to his reading public, *A Straightforward Tale*, a novella written shortly before he died in 1989, signals a return to his earlier fiction, particularly to *The Day of the Owl*. Again the irony of the story is implied by the title clearly aimed to satirize the impossibility to solve a murder organized and executed with the connivance of lay and religious authorities. *Chiesa Nostra* ("Our Church"), an ironic Sicilian adaptation of *Cosa Nostra* ("Our Thing") is meant to describe the alliance between powerful Catholic Church prelates and the Mafia, present in this tale of murder, drugs and betrayal.[11] At the conclusion Sciascia leaves the reader with the impression that a solution is nonexistent since civic and ecclesiastic authorities are the conspirators who betray the public trust.

The story, written in November 1989, establishes a feeling of bureaucratic ineptitude right at the start as a police Brigadier and an Inspector answer with reluctance a call from Giorgio Roccella, a retired diplomat who has returned to his villa in the Sicilian countryside after a long absence abroad. Roccella explains he must show without delay an unspecified thing he has found in his house. The call, however, is not deemed important enough by the police to justify an immediate follow-up. The Inspector sees no reason to give up a convivial evening with friends celebrating the feast of St. Joseph for a tedious excursion in the country. The trip to the villa next morning leads to the discovery of a corpse seated at a desk with a bullet in his head. The dead man is quickly identified as Giorgio Roccella. The alternatives are obvious. Either he has been murdered or he has committed suicide. Disregarding the objections of the Brigadier, the Chief Superintendent in charge of the investigation insists that the case is "straightforward" thus there is no need "to make too much of it."[12] As may be expected the case turns out to be far from straightforward not only for the people involved in the crime, but for the reader who is caught in a web of suspicions leading nowhere, while *carabinieri* ("special investigators") and authorities vie with each other to cover up the truth. The son and the former wife of the dead man arrive, the former from Stuttgart, the latter from Edinburgh adding an international twist to the story. It is agreed that a priceless canvas rolled up in a rug and stored in the attic must be blamed for the murder of the diplomat who, at the time he was shot, was looking forward to read what he considered his most valuable possession: two packets of letters, one bearing the signature of Garibaldi, the other of Pirandello. As the investigation proceeds readers are introduced to friends of Giorgio Roccella who enjoyed access to the villa, among them Father Cricco, "a striking man, tall and stern in his clerical attire" who declares himself an old fashioned Catholic who felt sorry for Roccella since he lacked "peace of heart." The skirmishes among police, relatives, investigators and the clergy proceed as the action evolves into a Pirandellian situation where everybody advances suspicions but is unable or unwilling to reach conclusions. Among the doubts, quarrels and Sciascia's conscious avoidance of essential details, a consensus is reached between the only two persons who seem to be on the right path: the police Brigadier and Professor Franco, a good friend of Roccella, as they privately discuss questionable details. The ability of the Inspector to locate at once the light switch to the stairs leading to the attic "behind the bust of St. Ignatius" for instance seems to indicate that the Inspector was familiar with the house. As the complexities multiply it becomes apparent that the painting is merely a decoy. It seems more probable that the inhabited villa has been used for other purposes and the refinery and storage of drugs are among the most likely suppositions. By turning up unexpectedly, Giorgio Roccella had signed his own death warrant.

In spite of the lack of evidence of a drug lab, a hint of its presence comes through as the Brigadier detects "a smell of something indefinable, perhaps burnt sugar, soaked eucalyptus leaves, or alcohol by the barns." The Inspector who accompanies him declines to acknowledge the smell, although he volunteers to bring in experts and dogs to assess the problem. To twist the plot even further, Sciascia introduces a fellow he identifies simply by the make of his car, the "Volvo man," a sort of contemporary everyman who happens to be an honest pharmaceutical representative–still dealing with drugs but legally–driving a Volvo on his way home. As he goes by a train dead on its tracks, he is asked the favor to go to the Monterosso Railroad Station to see what is the hold up. Once there he speaks with the Station Master who is watching two men rolling up a rug—the same rug, it seems, suspected of hiding the canvas stolen from the villa's attic but in all probability, packed with drugs. The "Volvo man" speaks with the stationmaster in charge of the two men who seem unhappy with the ordeal. As a matter of fact, once the stranger leaves they are promptly murdered. In a fast-moving scene as convincing as any Western shoot-out, the Brigadier fires against the Inspector in self-defense, thus eliminating the most dangerous accomplice of the mob since his highly placed position in the police force presented *Cosa Nostra* with an invaluable ally. A laconic headline in the daily paper reads: "Fatal Accident–Brigadier Cleaning Gun Shoots Inspector." Here, as in *Equal Danger*, the self-explanatory nature of the deed happily eliminates the necessity for an investigation. The Inspector is buried with the honors of his rank; the "Volvo man," under suspicion for the double murder in the Monterosso station, is released by the local police. As he is intent in making his way from the police station to his car, he runs into Father Cricco splendidly robed in ecclesiastic regalia on his way to the Inspector's funeral. The priest stops him to ask if by chance they had met before, or if he, still by chance to be sure, happened to be one of his parishioners. As he scrutinizes the features of the priest trying to remember where he has seen him before, the "Volvo man" firmly proclaims his lack of association with any parish. Suddenly, he remembers their previous encounter: "he was the stationmaster, or at least the one I took for the stationmaster." He is tempted to go back to the police and denounce him, but he decides against it. Instead he heads for his Volvo and drives away a free man at last, singing "at the top of his voice" in a long overdue emotional release. Songs at least are not incriminating. As for the rest, silence is the only way to avoid treacherous questions and stay alive. "A megghiu parola è chidda ca' un si dice" "The best word is the word that goes unsaid" is a Sicilian proverb that suits the "Volvo man" as he shuns the questions of Father Cricco and decides against going back to the police station to tell his side of the story. The casual reader may find the situation depicted in *A Straightforward Tale* clever, amusing, but hardly realistic. A statement from Judge Falcone, however, adds perspective to the story and shows that what may seem surrealistic satire on Sciascia's part, offers a penetrating insight into the unbelievable *imbrogli* ("complicated system") of Mafia machinations. Falcone writes:

> "The Mafia is not a cancer spreading by chance on a healthy organ. It lives in perfect symbiosis with a myriad of protectors, accomplices, informers, debtors of all kinds, high and low *maestri cantori* ("mastersingers") and people from every stratum of society who have been either intimidated or blackmailed. This is the terrain where *Cosa Nostra* thrives with all its direct and indirect implications acknowledged or unacknowledged, voluntary or imposed, often meeting with the approval of the people."[13]

Sciascia points with insistence to corruption in agencies meant to safeguard moral order and protect the rights of the civilian population: police, judges, and the clergy. The warning is clear. The law must guarantee equal justice for all or the tragic mockery that made the *Caso Moro* an indelible blot on the public conscience will find new victims as corrupted dignitaries consolidate their power and make the detection of abuses harder to identify. In writing his epitaph Sciascia captured the controversies he stirred during his life, controversies that went on even after his death: "Ce ne ricorderemo di questo mondo," "We will remember this world." The epitaph can be read as a warning that the writer's tireless fight against hypocrisy and social abuses would not end with his death. Sciascia's controversial political pronouncements often marked by sarcastic innuendos serve as reminder of the writer's civic courage and of his tireless resolve to face criticism for what he considered the right cause. Few would question that the world remembers him—*Cosa*

Nostra included. No Sicilian writer before or after Sciascia has cast more light in the tradition of men of honor, their ruthless fight for dominance, the hypocrisy of the political untouchables who use the Mafia to carry out the only straightforward promise they mean to keep: the growth and the stability of the family business.

VII

The Mafia Today

While assessing the Mafia's longevity Giuffrida De Felice, well known authority on the subject, explains: "this social plague [the Mafia] was born from a burning, wide spread, irresistible thirst for economic, political, social justice."[1] Francesco Renda, senator from Agrigento, echoes De Felice's view when he remarks:

> "Mafioso signifies a given moral attitude of instinctive and moral rebellion against an existing system that is disintegrating. It is the elementary expression of a citizen who does not see in the extant society a guarantee for his personal safety or the safety of his possessions nor a fair administration of justice."

When journalist Saverio Lodato asked Alfonso Giordano, judge in the maxi-trial of *Cosa Nostra* (1986): "What will the Mafia become in the year 2000?" Giordano replied: "It will be a Mafia running on computers, telex, high finance, financial subsidiaries. The Mafia has always been successful in transforming itself according to the needs of the time" [2]

While judge Giordano's reply to Lodato offers a bleak forecast of things to come, Francesco Renda's comment is based on his reaction to the mistreatment Sicilians suffered through various occupations, a factor that contributed to developing a deeply rooted feeling of distrust. Many young Sicilians, mostly students, are receptive to new ideas and ready to break with the past. Although their good intentions are tested constantly, they realize that perseverance is indispensable to eliminate Mafioso's influence from public life. The Mafia in power (*alta Mafia*) still has leverage and keeps running business with characteristic opportunism taking advantage of a tradition embedded in the culture and therefore difficult to eradicate.

Writers of plays and novels discussed here followed historical and cultural indicators unveiling implications behind the facade. The determination of the Sicilian aristocracy to secure political clout in the new government in Rome finds its avatar in the historical pragmatism of Prince Consalvo in De Roberto's *I Vicerè*, where, anticipating Tancredi's Machiavellian shrewdness in Lampedusa's *The Leopard*, Consalvo, the prince politician, warns his aunt Donna Ferdinanda: "history is a monotonous repetition; mankind has been, is, and will always be the same," a sentiment Tancredi will make even more explicit in *The Leopard* as he tells his uncle, Prince Salina, what seems a truism, but in reality is nothing more than a clever syllogism: "If we want things stay as they are, things will have to change." Tancredi's mandate, incidentally, still finds fulfillment in the Mafia's political versatility and in the *onorata società*'s remarkable talent for adapting to contemporary needs.

In a subtly different key Pirandello's *I Vecchi e I Giovani* ("The Old and the Young") tells how the growing disillusionment with a corrupt political system destroyed the idealism of the Italian *Risorgimento* and allowed a coup by self-gratifying politicians who left the ultra-conservative Mafia take advantage of the disappointment of the patriots and of the emerging labor unions in order to consolidate their power in the new administration. Pirandello's skeptical view of the law, ready to punish but never able to come to the aid of the beleaguered citizen, helps explain why in such climate of distrust the *famiglia* became a protective association of individuals bound by shared interests and by common goals. It explains as well the glorification of the Mafioso in movie plots where Mafiosi often have been shown as champions of traditional values.

In his plays, *Violence* and *Ultimate Violence*, Giuseppe Fava indicts a judicial system that has favored wealthy Mafiosi represented in court by lavishly paid lawyers. The intention of these plays is not so much to present the advantages enjoyed by well connected godfathers–arguably an everyday occurrence in Italian courts–as to bring to the attention of the public the shameful slavery imposed on petty criminals who carry out orders for the mob in order to survive. Power begets power, Fava implies, and the law is on the side of the powerful even when the powerful undermine the role of justice.

Leonardo Sciascia's presentation of the long forgotten comedy *La Mafia* as a relevant example of Mafioso ingenuity or, more appropriately, as a Magna Carta of Mafioso pragmatism, offers a candid evaluation of Sicily's unresolved problems. The fact is that Mafioso behavior is part of a long-standing tradition that cannot be easily dismissed. As Sicilian literature implies, solutions do not come easily. The key to Sciascia's view of the Mafia is his exposure and condemnation of criminal behavior. Since he evaluates the situation in its cultural and historic context, he joins Fava in accusing authorities of persecuting minor members of the *onorata società* and ignoring powerful *padrini*. Sciascia is too Sicilian to probe the intricate issues the Mafia poses by relying exclusively on his instinct as a writer. Even when tempered by sarcasm his tales reach beyond the evaluation of facts to fathom the inscrutable depths of human motivation. His goal is apparent in all major works of political or fictional content, unquestionably in *The Moro Affair* and *The Day of the Owl*.

Today few experts on the subject would deny that the Mafia is losing its unique cultural identity. Some traces of the tradition can be found in the nostalgic longing for times gone by still evident in the stories of the repentant Mafiosi. Following the lead of *il grande pentito*, Don Masino Buscetta, they share revelations often padded with details made to order for a public with an insatiable appetite for mob stories. At this point in time the literature of the Mafia in Italy as well as in the United States consists mostly of memoirs written or dictated by loquacious Mafiosi who dedicate their long days in prison or in federal witness programs to narrate their exploits. What distinguishes these stories–usually written with the help of capable professionals–is the narrative tone filled with suspense, thrilling descriptions and the Mafiosi's unmistakable desire to establish their version of the truth.

While Sciascia remains the uncontested master of Sicilian Mafia narrative due to the insights he brings to the topic, as we have seen in the United States Mario Puzo's *The Godfather* stands as a nostalgic reminder of a Sicilian tradition that persists in television like *The Sopranos* and the American legend of the self-made man, a lasting stereotype of the rags-to-riches myth in the land of opportunity. Max Weber in *Economy and Society* writes:

> "It would be interesting to compare protection money [demanded by the Mafia] with insurance premiums: here also we pay regularly and in the majority of cases we receive no service in return because we (fortunately) do not need it or because the insurer avoids payment." [3]

As for the Sicilians, they do not seem inclined to change, often with reason. A persistent hostility toward the *mezzogiorno* (southern Italians) and the inadequate way the Italian government meets the many needs of the people in southern Italy perpetuate the conditions portrayed by Sciascia and other writers who present with understandable sarcasm a problem crying for a solution. It is important, however, to expose the evil of the Mafia without confusing its criminal liabilities with Sicilian traditions. Franco Ferrotti, professor of Sociology at the University of Rome, writes:

> "Psychological values and attitudes of an essentially Mafioso kind are so wide spread [in Sicily] that by those who lived immersed in them they are not explicitly recognized as such. We have arrived at a paradox. People and social groups that live in an environment dominated by Mafioso values, deny with the utmost naturalness the existence of the Mafia. They cannot see modern society and their own

everyday experience except through those values. But they don't realize this, so 'natural' do those values appear."⁴

These values accepted as a way of life and treated by Sicilian writers as a relevant aspect of their culture are intriguing enough to captivate readers understandably challenged by what seem, and often is, a series of contradictions. Sorting out details in these narratives is not for those who look for easy answers.

Still a question remains. Does a growing awareness of the dangers posed by the Mafia spur an effort to eliminate the *onorata società*? Today the *cupola* or the Mafia's high command is assessing its position while testing opportunities to consolidate business and political alliances in operations hardly distinguishable from legitimate practices. The goal is easy enough to achieve in the age of cyberspace. Authors of social studies, of fictionalized Mafia stories and movie producers who, along with the press, monitor these trends may do well to turn their attention to unexpected developments. They should recall warnings in medieval maps posted to indicate danger in territories yet unexplored: *hic sunt leones* ("here are the lions"). As for Sicilian writers, it must be admitted that either through undeniable knowledge or subtle implication they never hesitated to show the dangerous realities of Sicilian life and the burden endured by a people caught in the dichotomy of passive submission and bloody revenge.

Notes

Chapter I

[1] Giovanni Cucinotta. Dove, Quando, Perche, Mafia. Cosenza: Pellegrini Editore, pp. 41-42. Alll translations from the Italian unless differently stated are by this writer.

[2] Henner Hess. Mafia and Mafiosi: Origin, Power, and Myth. Translated by Ewald Osers. New York University Press, 1998, p.80.

[3] Antonio Cuterera. La mafia ed I Mafiosi. Origine e manifestazioni. Studio di Sociologia Criminale Palermo, 1990.

[4] Giovanni Cucinotta. Mafia: Dove, Quandro, Perchè. p. 30.

[5] Giovanni Cuinotta, p. 31.

[6] Henner Hess writes: "In official documents of the past century the terms mafiosi and camorristi are still used indiscriminately. It is thought that the camorra originated in the 14th century--'compagnia quae fuit in Kallari dicta de Gamurra'--[company that was in Kallari and was called Gamurra]. The name has been derived from the Arabic Kumar, the game of dice forbidden by the Koran, or from the Arabic gamara, the place where such gaming takes place." (Mafia and Mafiosi, p. 101).

[7] Michele Pantaleone. Mafia e droga. Torino: Rizzoli, 1983.

[8] Leonardo Sciascia. The Day of the Owl. Translated from the Italian by A. Colquhoun & A. Oliver. Boston: David Godine, 1984, pp. 87-88.

[9] Alfredo Giovanni Cesareo. La Mafia, as quoted by Leonardo Sciascia in La Letteratura sulla Mafia, Roma: Bonacci Editore, 1998, p. 39.

[10] Giovanni Falcone, his wife and several members of his escort were killed in 1994 while driving to Palermo by a blast of 100 Kgs. of TNT.

[11] Giovanni Falcone with Marcelle Padovani. Cose di Cosa Nostra. Milano: 1991, p. 86.

[12] Leonardo Sciascia. La Vita Quotidiana dell Mafia dal 1950 a Oggi. Introduction. Milano: Biblioteca Universale Rizzoli, 1986, p. 52.

[13] Vittorio Fronsini. "Mitologia e Sociologia dell Mafia" La Mafia: QuattroStudi. Bologna: Massimiliano Boni: Editore, 1970, pp. 7-32.

[14] Cited in Giovonni Falcone. Cose di Cosa Nostra. Tu collaborazione cou Marcelle Padovani. Milano: Rizzoli, 1991. p. 43.

[15] Rocco Chinnici, La Vita Quotidiana della Mafia dal 1950 a Oggi. Milano: Bilblioteca Universale Rizzoli, p. 35.

[16] Giovanni Cucinotta, p. 34.

[17] All quotations of "Violence" are from La Letteratura sulla Mafia. Roma: Bonacci Editone. 1998, pp. 99-102.

[18] Fabrizio Calvi. LaVita Quotidiana della Mafia dal 1950 a Oggi, p. 33.

[19] Joseph Bonanno with Sergio Lolli. A Man of Honor: The Autobiography of Joseph Bonanno. New York: Simon and Schuster, 1983, p. 297.

[20] Joseph Bonanno, p. 271.

[21] Leonardo Sciascia. Open Doors and Three Novellas. Translated by Joseph Farrel. New York: Alfred Knopf, 1992.

Chapter II

[1] Giovanni Cucinotta. Mafia. Dove, Quandro, Perchè, p. 14.
[2] Mafia. Dove, Quattro, Perchè, p. 17.
[3] Mafia. Dove, Quattro, Perchè, p. 21.
[4] Mafia. Dove, Quattro, Perchè, p. 25.
[5] A Man of Honor, p. 3.
[6] Carlo Levi, "Le parole sono pietre" La lettteratura sulla Mafia. Roma: BonaccI, 1988, p. 77.
[7] Giovanni Verga, I Malavoglia. Milano: Mondadori, 1970, p. 228.
[8] Giuseppe Quadriglio, A Thousand Years in Sicily. translated by Justin Vitello. New York: Legas, 1991, pp. 291-224.
[9] Giuseppe Fava. Mafia. Da Giuliani a Dalla Chiesa. Roma: Editori Riuniti, 1984, p. 11.
[10] Leonardo Sciascia, "Mafia," La Vita Quotidiana della Mafia, pp. 14-15.
[11] Saverio Lodato. Venti Anni di Mafia. Milano: Rizzoli, 1999, p. 337.
[12] The allusion is to movie techniques.
[13] Venti Anni di Mafia, p. 333.

Chapter III

[1] Vittorio Frosini, "Mitologia e Sociologia della Mafia" La Mafia, Quattro Studi. Bologna: Massimiliano Boni Editore, 1970, p. 15.
[2] Vittorio Frosini. "Mitologia e Sociologia della Mafia," La Mafia: Quattro Studi, p. 17.
[3] Henner Hess. Mafia, Mafiosi. Origin, Power, and Myth, p. 191.
[4] Frandesco Crispi (1819-1901) Italian statesman, was Premiere for two terms: 1887-1891; 1893-1896.
[5] Commedia dell'arte. A type of comedy characterized by improvisation on a three acts scenario. The roles were assigned to actors who specialized in the parts they played. The most famous were the Venetian Pantalone, the Bolognese Don Graziano, the Bergamasco Arlecchino, the Neapolitan Punch and Judy. The first troupe of Comedians was formed in 1545. The Comedians traveled to various countries, greatly influencing the European stage.
[6] In Sicilian calamari, inkwell. Iachinu is referring to the newspaper The Incognito is reading.
[7] Giuseppe Rizzotto. I Mafiusi di la Vicaria di Palermo. Introduction, Salvatore Pedone. Palermo:Editrice Reprint, S.A.S
[8] Leonardo Sciascia, I Mafiosi. Torino: Milano: Adelphi Edizioni, 1991.

Chapter IV

[1] Italo Calvino Fiabe Italiane, Vol. II. Milano: Oscar Mondadori, 1980.
[2] Michele La Tona, La vera storia della Baronessa di Carini. Palermo: Antares Editrice, 1997, p. 10.
[3] "L'arte di Franceschiello" Fiabe Italiane. Transcribed by Italo Calvino. Vol. II. Milano: Oscar Mondadori, 1980, pp. 430-36.

⁴ Arciprete is composed by arc. principal, and prete, priest. Corruption among priests was widespread in Sicily often encouraged and justified by legislation as the Taxae cancellariae et penitentiaries romanae imposed by the archbishop of Palermo, Giovan Battista dei Conti Naselli, between 1477-1533. The law favored churchmen, who were considered part of the elite class. Criminal charges against them were usually dismissed even if the implications included false testimony in court.

⁵ Even today mettere nel sacco, to put someone inside a sack, means to fool someone who is not aware of what is going on.

⁶ Leonardo Sciascia. Le parroacchie di Regalpetra. Milano: Adelphi. 1991, p. 41.

⁷ Luigi Capuana, "The Bond of San Giovanni." Stories of Sicily. Translated by A. Alexander. New York: Schoken Books, 1975, p.64.

⁸ Luigi Capuana, "The Bond of San Giovanni," p13.

⁹ Luigi Capuana, "The Bond of San Giovanni," p. 36

¹⁰ In other parts of Italy Don precedes the name of a priest.

¹¹ Leonardo Sciascia, The Day of the Owl, p. 95.

¹² Luigi Capuana, Carteggio Verga-Capuana a cura di S. Zappulla Muscarà. Catania. 1973.

¹³ Giovanni Verga. The House by the Medlar Tree. Translated by R. Rosenthal. Berkeley: University of California Press, 1964. All the quotations that follow are from the same edition.

¹⁴ The House by the Medlar Tree, p. 228.

¹⁵ The House by the Medlar Tree, p. 236.

¹⁶ Leonardo Sciascia. The Day of the Owl, p. 36.

¹⁷ Leonardo Sciascia, Pirandello e la Sicilia. Milano: Adelphi Edizioni, 1996, p.29.

¹⁸ Giovanni Verga. Mastro Don Gesualdo. Translated by Giovanni Cecchetti. Berkeley: University of California Press, 1984, p.147. All quotations are from this text.

Chapter V

¹ The reference is to the 19th century movement that brought about the unification of Italy.

² Ugo Ojetti, well known journalist and critic, collaborated with Milano's Corriere della Sera where he was editor from 1925 to 1927.

³ Luigi Pirandello, I Vecchi e I Giovani. Acure di Anna Nozzoli. Milano: Mondadori, 1992, p.xiii

⁴ Leonardo Sciascia. Pirandello e la Sicilia, pp. 72-74.

⁵ Luigi Pirandello. I Vecchi e I Giovani, p.97-98.

⁶ Federico De Roberto. I Vicere. Milano: Mondadori, 2000, pp. 281-284.

⁷ Federico De Roberto. I Vicere. pp. 281-282

⁸ I Vicerè. p. 636.

⁹ I Vicerè. p. 674.

¹⁰ Nicolo Machiavelli. The Prince. The Portable Machiavelli. Edited by P. Bondanella and M. Musa. New York: Penguin, 1979, p. 160.

¹¹ Nicolo Machiavelli. The Discourses. The Portable Machiavelli, p. 192.

[12] Frosini, Renda, Sciascia. La Mafia. Quattro Studi. Bologna: Massimo Boni, Editore, 1970, p. 54.
[13] Giovanni Verga. Mastro Don Gesusldo. trans by Giovanni Cecchetti. Berkeley: Univ. of California Press, 1984, p.27.
[14] Tomasi di Lampedusa. The Leopard. Translated by A. Colquhoun. New York: Pantheon, 1960, p. 261.
[15] Lampedusa, The Leopard, p. 40.
[16] Lampedusa, The Leopard, p. 88.
[17] Luigi Pirandello. I Vecchi e I Giovani, p. 490.
[18] Lampedusa, The Leopard, p.320.
[19] Lampedusa. The Leopard, p. 45.
[20] Lampedusa The Leopard, p. 17.
[21] Lampedusa. The Leopard, p. 46-47.
[22] Lampedusa. The Leopard, p. 81.
[23] The names chosen by Lampedusa refer to the epics of Ludovico Arioso (1474-1533) and Torquato Tasso (11544-1595) still popular in Sicilian tradition. Tancredi is the hero of Tasso's Gerusalemme Liberata, Jerusalem Delivered, while Angelica is the heroine of Ariosto's Orlando Furioso always running away from her suitors. Donnafugata, the name of the Salina's villa, means "woman abducted," a further reminder of Ariosto's heroine.
[24] Lampedusa. The Leopard, p. 21-169.
[25] Plebiscite derives from the Latin plebs, people, and scitum, from scire, to know. It means: to seek the will of the people.
[26] Lampedusa, The Leopard, p. 128.
[27] Lampedusa. The Leopard, p. 132.
[28] Lampedusa. The Leopard, 203-206.
[29] Lampedusa. The Leopard, pp. 209-210.

Chapter VI

[1] The Brigate Rosse, Red Brigades, at first were a result of working class rebellion against unfair labor practices. They originated in 1970 in Milan and relied mostly on strikes often accompanied by violence and sabotage. Although these rebellious acts were frequently promoted by the dissatisfaction of immigrants from southern Italy often victims of local prejudice, most members of the movement were not associated with Lotta Continua, Continuing Struggle, the core of the group. It relied instead on Labor organizers and on veterans of the 1969 student movement who, by now, were on the faculty of Social Studies at the University of Trento. In order to wage a more effective war against those they saw as enemies of the people, they chose to operate from the underground. After their leader, Renato Curcio, was arrested a second time in 1974, Mario Moretti succeeded him. It was then that the worst aspects of terrorism broke out. State attorney Francesco Coco, for instance, was murdered for his failure to trade eight members of the Brigate Rosse scheduled to go on trial for Mario Sossi, a magistrate held hostage by the terrorists.
[2] The New York Review of Books, June 25, 1987.
[3] Giovanni Falcone. Cose di Cosa Nostra, p. 167.

⁴ Leonardo Sciascia. Le Parrocchie di Regalpetru. Milano: Aldelphi, 1991, p.11.

⁵ Leonardo Sciascia. The Day of the Owl, p. 13.

⁶ Saverio Lodato. Venti Anni di Mafia. Milano: Rizzoli, 1999.

⁷ All quotations from Leonardo Sciascia: The Day of the Owl are from Godine Double Detectives, edited by Robin w. Winks, David Godine Publisher: Boston, 1984.

⁸ Leonardo Sciascia. The Day of the Owl. Afterward, viii.

⁹ This is an "in" joke on Sciascia's part. Bitter vermuth or Cinar is extracted from the artichoke–carciofo in Italian, cosca in Sicilian–symbol of the Mafia. The vegetable has become symbol of the politica del carciofo, or Mafia politics.

¹⁰ Equal Danger. Boston: Godine, 1984, p. 119.

¹¹ The Sicilian Catholic clergy, especially in Monreale, near Palermo, has been repeatedly suspected of collaborating with the Mafia by showing an open favoritism tor powerful construction interests. The behavior of the former bishop of Monreale, Monsignor Salvator Cassisa, justifies the claim. According to pentito Li Pera, Monsignor Cassisa received a gift of 600 million lire from the Rizzani De Eccher Construction Company for awarding the firm a contract to repair the Arab-Norman cathedral of Monreale. His lucrative alliance with powerful Mafiosi in the construction business became well known. His personal secretary, Don (Reverend in this case) Mario Campisi, favored the activities of Leoluca Bagarella, one of Corleone's most dangerous bosses. Warnings from the Vatican–some too vague to be effective–even the visit of Pope John Paul to Palermo (1992) did not alter the situation. As Saverio Lodato,correspondent for the communist paper L'Unita in Sicily,explains in Chiesa Nostra, Our Church, " there will be no complete freedom of the church from the Mafia until a bishop will be able to defy simultaneously the investigationsof the magistrates, the profound uneasiness of the faithful, the choices of the high ecclesiastical hierarchies." For more documentation on the involvement of the Sicillian Catholic Church with Cosa Nostra see Saverio Lodato, Venti anni di Mafia: C'era una volta la lotta alla Mafia. Milano: Rizzoli, Saggi Superbur, 1999, pp. 343-350.

¹² Leonardo Sciascia. "A Straightforward Tale" Open Doors and Three Novellas. Translated by Joseph Farrell. New York: Alfred Knopf, 1992, p. 167.

¹³ Giovanni Falcone. Cosde di Cosa Nostra. p 16.

Chapter VII

¹ Giuffrida De Felice as quoted by Francesco Renda in La Mafia: Quattro Studi della Mafia. Bologna: Massimiliano Boni, 1970, p. 43, footnote 6.

² Saverio Lodato, Venti Anni di Mafia, p. 223.

³ citied from Henner Hess. Mafia and Mafiosi, p. 196, footnote 17.

⁴ Franco Ferrotti. "The Sicilian Mafia, 1860-1977" Italian Journal. New York: 1989, no. 5, Vol. III, pp. 17-28.

Works cited

Primary Sources

Alexander, Shana. *The Pizza Connections*. New York: Widened & Nicolson, 1988.
Ambroise, Cl;aude. "Les Traces de Vie," *L' Arc*. Paris, Fall 1987.
Badalamenti, Rev. Vincenzo. *Il Castello e la Baronessa di Carini*. Palermo: Edizioni Belllanca, 1995.
Bonanno, Joseph, with Serfio Lolli. *A Man of Honor. The Autobiography of Joseph Bonanno*. New York: Simon and Schuster, 1983.
Bonanno, Bill. *Bound by Honor*. New York: St. Martin's Press, 2000.
Brydone, Patrick. *A Tour through Sicily and Malta in a Series of Letters to William Beckford, Esq, in Frosini, Renda, Sciascia, La Mafia*. Bologna: Massimiliano Boni, 1970.
Calvi, Fabrizio. *La Vita Quotidiana della Mafia dal 1950 a Oggi*. Milano: Rizzoli, 1986.
Calvino, Italo. *L'Arte di Franceschiello in Fiabe Italiane, II*. Milano: Oscar Mondadori, 1956.
Capuana, Luigi. *The Bond of San Giovanni* transl. by A. Alexander. *In Stories of Sicily*. New York: Schoken Books, 1975.
Costanzo, Angelo. *Giuf': The Fool of Sicily* in *Arba Sicula*, XIV (Spring and Fall 1993): 45-59.
Croce, Benedetto. *Filosofia della Pratica*. Bari: Laterza, 1909.
Cucinotta, Giovanni. *Mafia: Dove, Quando, Perche*. Cosenza: Pellegrini Editore, 1987.
De Roberto, Federico. *I Vicere*. Milano: Mondadori, 1991.
Dizionario geografico, statistico e biografico della Sicilia. Palermo, 1819.
Eco, Umberto. *Introduction to Luigi Natoli's Grande romanzo storico siciliano*. 2 Vols. Palermo: Flaccovio, 1974.
Falcone, Giuseppe with Marcelle Padovani. *Cose di Cosa Nostra*. Milano: Rizzoli Libri S.p.A, 1991.
Fava, Giuseppe. *Mafia: Da Giuliano a Dalla Chiesa*. Roma: Editori Riuniti, 1986.
Fentress, James. *Rebels and Mafiosi*. Ithaca: Cornell University Press, 2000.
Ferrarotti, Franco. "The Sicilian Mafia: 1860-1977" in *Italian Journal*, New York, vol. III, no.5.

Works cited

Frosini, Vittorio. *Mitologia e Sociologia della Mafia in La Mafia*. Quattro Studi. Bologna: Massimiliano Boni, 1970.
Galasso, Alfredo. *La Mafia non esiste*. Napoli: Pironti, 1988.
Hess, Henner. *Mafia and Mafiosi. Origin, Power and Myth*. Trans. by Ewald Osers. New York University Press, 1998.
Hobsbawn, E. J. *Primitive Rebels. Studies in Archaic Forms of Social Movements in the 19th and 20th Centuries*. Manchester University Press, 1959.
Janni, Francis A.J. with Elizabeth Reuss Janni. *A Family Business. Kinship and Social Control in Organized Crime*. New York: New American Library, 1972.
Kelly, Robert, Cooperation Between Italian and American Enforcement Agencies. "The Fight Against Organized Crime" *Italian Journal*, III, (No. 2-3), 1989.
Lampedusa, Giuseppe. *The Leopard*. Tr. by A. Colquhoun. New York: Pantheon, 1960.
La Duca, Rosario. *Almanacco Popolare Palermitano*. Palermo: Edizioni e Ristampe Siciliane, 1980.
La Tona, Michele. *La vera storia della Baronessa di Carini*. Palermo. Antares Editrice: 1997.
Levi,Carlo. *Le parole sono pietre in La letteratura della Mafia*. Roma: Bonacci, 1988.
Lodato, Saverio. *Venti Anni di Mafia. C'era una volta la lotta alla Mafia*. Milano: Rizzoli, Superbur Saggi, 1999.
Maas, Peter. *Underboss. Sammy the Bull Gravano's Story of Life in the Mafia*. New York: Harper Collins, 1997.
Machiavelli, Nicoloi. *The Prince, The Discourses in The Portable Machiavelli*. Trans. by P. Bondanella & M. Musa. New York: Penguin, 1983.
Mori, Cesare. *The Last Struggle with the Mafia*. Trans. by Orlo Williams. London and New York: Putnam, 1933.
Muscetta, Carlo. *Letteratura di Mafia in La letteratura sulla Mafia*. Roma: Bonacci Editore, 1988.
Pirandello, Luigi. *I vecchi e i giovani, a cura di Anna Nozzoli*. Milano: Mondadori, 1992.
_____*Il fu Mattia Pascal*. Milano: Mondadori, 1946.
_____*Naked Masks: Five Plays*. Edited by Eric Bentley. New York: Dutton & Co. Inc., 1952.
Pitre', Giuseppe. *Usi e costumi credenze e pregiudizi del popolo siciliano*. Vol. II. Palermo, 1889.
Renard, Philippe. "Les Lunettes de Sciascia" in *L'Arc*, Paris (34).
Renda, Francesco. *Funzioni e basi sociali della Mafia. La Mafia*. Quattro Studi.Bologna: Massimiliano Boni, 1970.
Rizzotto, Giuseppe. *I Mafiusi di la Vicaria di Palermu*. Palermo: Editrice Reprint 1994.
Schifano, Jean Noel. "Sciascia ou de la candeur" in *L'Arc,* Paris. 1996.
Sciascia, Leonardo. *The Day of the Owl*. Trans. by Archibald Colquhoun & Arthur Oliver; *Equal Danger*. Trans. by Adrianne Foulke. Afterward by Frank Kermode. Boston: Godine Double Detective, 1984.
_____*Appunti su Mafia e Letteratura in La Mafia. Quattro Studi*. Bologna: Massimiliano Boni, 1970.
_____*Pirandello e la Sicilia*. Milano: Adelphi, 1996.

____*A ciascuno il suo*. Edited by Iole Fiorillo Magri. Boston: Houghton Mifflin, 1976.
____*Todo Modo*. Torino: Giulio Einaudi, 1974.
____*A Straightforward Tale* in *Open Doors and three novellas*. Trans. by Joseph Farrell. New York: Alfred Knopf, 1992.
Stille, Alexander. *Excellent Cadavers. The Mafia and the Death of the First Italian Republic*. New York: Random House, 1996.
Quadriglio, Giuseppe. *A Thousand Years in Sicily*. Translated by Justin Vitello. New York: Legas, 1991.
Verga, Giovanni. "Cavalleria Rusticana Comparaggio". Trans. by Alfred Alexander in *Stories of Sicily*. New York: Schoken Books, 1975.
____ *I Malavoglia*. Milano: Mondadori, 1970.
____*The House by the Medlar Tree*. Trans. by Raymond Rosenthal. Berkeley: U. of California Press, 1983.
____*Mastro Don Gesualdo*. Trans. by Giovanni Cecchetti. Berkeley: U. of California Press, 1984. *Vocabolario Siciliano-Italiano*. Palermo: Editrie Reprin, 1994.

General Bibliography

Arlacchi, Pino. *La mafia imprenditrice*. Bologna, 1983.
____*Addio Cosa Nostra*. Milano, 1994.
Blumenthal, Ralph. *The Last Days of the Sicilians*. New York, 1988.
Caponetto, Antonio with Lodati, Saverio. *I miei giorni a Palermo*. Milano, 1992.
Colajanni, Napoleone. *Nel regno della Mafia [1900]*. Catanzaro, 1984.
Dalla Chiesa, Nando. *Delitto Imperfetto*. Milano, 1984.
Di Fonzo, Luigi. *St. Peter's Banker: Michele Sindona*. New York, 1983.
Duggan, Christopher. *Fascism and the Mafia*. New Haven, 1989.
Fava, Claudio. *La mafia comanda a Catania: 1960-1991*. Roma-Bari, 1991.
Fentress, James and Chris Wickham. *Social Memory*. Oxford, 1992.
Franchetti, Leopoldo. *Condizioni politiche e amministrative della Sicilia [1887]*. Roma, 1992.
Gambetta, Diego. *The Sicilian Mafia*. Cambridge, 1993.
Ginzburg, Paul. *A History of Contemporary Italy*. New York, 1990.
La Masa, Giuseppe. *Documenti della rivoluzione siciliana del 1847-49 in rapporto all'Italia*. Torino, 1850.
Lazzari Santi. *La mafia*. Messina, 1892.
Lea, Charles Henry. *The Inquisition in the Spanish Dependencies*. New York, 1908.
Mack Smith, Denis. *Cavour and Garibaldi*. Cambridge, 1985 [Reprint}.
____*A History of Sicily*. 2 vols. London, 1969.
Mangiameli, Rosario. *Le allegorie del buon governo: sui rapporti fra Mafia e Americani in Sicilia nel 1943*. Facoltà di Scienze Politiche, Università di Catania, 1981.
Maraini, Dacia. *Bagheria*. Milano, 1993.
Mazzanuto, Pietro. *La mafia nella letterataura*. Palermo, 1970.
Messanan, Eugenio N. *Racalmuto nella storia di Sicilia*. Canicatti, 1969.
Mori, Cesare. *Con la mafia ai ferri corti. [1932]*. Palermo, 1993.
Mosca, Gaetano. *The Ruling Class*. Trans. Hannah D. Kahn. New York, 1939.

Nelli, Humbert S. *The Business of Crime*. New York, 1976.
Novacco, Domenico. *L'inchiesta sulla Mafia*. Milano, 1963.
Orlando, Leoluca. *Palermo*. Milano, 1990.
Pantaleone, Michele. *Mafia e politica*. Torino, 1960.
____*Anti-mafia occasione perduta*. Torino,1969.
____*A cavallo della tigre*. Palermo, 1984.
Pilo, Rosolino. "Esatta cronaca dei fatti avvenuti in Sicilia". *Il Risorgimento Italiano*, vol. 7, no.1 (January-February) pp. 1-25.
Rampollo, Giovanni. *Suicidio per Mafia*. Palermo, 1986.
Renda, Francesco. *Storia della Sicilia*. Palermo: vol. I, 1984; vol. II, 1985; vol. III, 1987.
____*I beati paoli*. Palermo, 1988.
Romano, S.F. *Storia dei Fasci siciliani*. Bari, 1959.
Scalici, Emanuele. *La mafia siciliana*. Palermo, 1984 [reprint].
Stajano, Corrado. *L'atto di accusa dei giudici di Palermo*. Roma, 1986.
(Reprints of sentenza ordinanza contro Abbate + 706 indictment of the ordinance filed in Palermo November 8, 1985, mostly conceived by judges Giovanni Falcone e Paolo Borsellino).
Sterling, Claire. *Octopus*. New York, 1990.
Titone, Virgilio. *Considerazioni sulla Mafia in Scienze giuridiche, politiche e sociali*. Palermo, 1957.
Tommasi-Crudeli, T. *La Sicilia in 1871*. Firenze.
Trevelyan, G. M. *Garibaldi and the Thousand*. London, 1909.
Uccello, A. *Carcere e mafia nei canti popolari siciliani*. Roma, 1974.
Winnington, Ingram H.F. *Hearts of Oak*. London, 1889.

www.ingramcontent.com/pod-product-compliance
Lightning Source LLC
Chambersburg PA
CBHW032300150426
43195CB00008BA/523